The Quotable Tennis Player

Edited by
Scott Perlstein

THE LYONS PRESS
Guilford, Connecticut
An imprint of The Globe Pequot Press

The Library of Congress Cataloging-in-Publication Data ia available on file.

ISBN 1-58574-660-6
Manufactured in the United States of America

10 9 8 7 6 5 4 3 2 1

Contents

Introduction   1

History of the Game   3

Training and Preparation   27

For the Love of the Game   41

The State of the Game   65

Humor On and Off the Court   97

The Tournaments   129

The Players   141

The Mind Game   215

The Thrill of Victory . . .   251

Wisdom and Advice from the Pros   265

Unforgettable Moments   299

Bibliography   313

Index   319

Acknowledgments

I would like to thank Jennifer Oshita, Daisy Dupont, Heromi Nakano, and Roland Bardony for helping load quotes into the computer, and my wife, Karen, for helping find the quotes, for loading them into the computer, and for editing.

Abbreviations

The following abbreviations are used throughout this book and are spelled out here for readers who may not be familiar with them:

ATP   Association of Tennis Professionals
WTA   Women's Tennis Association
ITF   International Tennis Federation
USTA   United States Tennis Association
USLTA   United States Lawn Tennis Association (former name of the USTA)
USPTA   United States Professional Tennis Association

Introduction

Tennis is a great sport, both for the participants and for those on the sidelines. It is exciting to watch but also offers players a lifetime of participation. One can live anywhere in the world, play at any level, and always find people to compete against. Watching tennis at the pro level, whether in person or on television, can be a great teaching tool, not to mention great fun.

Tennis is an international sport played in and televised to all parts of the world. In many countries the tennis pros are some of the most famous people. For example, Boris Becker of Germany, Yannick Noah of France, and Gustavo Kuerten of Brazil are all national heroes.

The game of tennis has enjoyed a long and rich history. To compile this book, I searched for interesting, memorable, and educational quotes in the hope that readers would gain a varied perspective on the game and a deep appreciation of this incredible sport.

I searched Web sites of the major tournaments for player interviews, found the Web sites of many of the current top pros, and consulted libraries and bookstores for the best material (my own library has now grown significantly!). I tracked down many memorable moments in tennis history and tried to find the corresponding thoughts of the people who were present on these occasions.

More than three hundred people are quoted in this book: Players from the very early days of tennis to the present, writers on the sport, observers of the sport, and even some relative unknowns are found here. Although I tried to be comprehensive, I may have unintentionally left some exceptional individuals out of the book, and I apologize for these oversights.

I hope you enjoy this collection of quotations about the greatest sport in the world.

History of the Game

Louis X of France was the first royal patron of the early game of tennis. Although some believe he was poisoned in 1318, one of the early myths of tennis is that he died from exhaustion after an extremely strenuous game.

CYNDY MUSCUTEL
"The Past: From Monks to Monarchs," *World Tennis Ratings* Web site, Winter 2001

Henry VII may have contributed the word "service" to the game by having a man-servant put the ball in play.

CHRISTOPHER DUNKLEY
Tennis: Nostalgia, Playing the Game

On June 17, three days after the court reached Marly, the third estate declared itself unilaterally to be a National Assembly and that it was with the intent of providing a new constitution. On June 20, locked out of the usual salon in which they met, the deputies adjourned to one of Versailles' tennis courts and a general oath was administrated. This oath ignored the theoretical powers of the monarch. This became known as the tennis court oath.

ANTONIA FRASER
Marie Antoinette: The Journey

When we have march'd our rackets to these balls
We will, in France, by God's grace, play a set,
Shall strike his father's crown into the hazard.
Tell him he hath made a match with such a
    wrangler—
That all the courts of France will be disturbed

        WILLIAM SHAKESPEARE
        Henvy V

In 1874 the modern game of tennis was invented but it goes back in some form for centuries. Kings have played it. Chaucer, Shakespeare and many other early writers described it. In the fourteenth and fifteenth centuries primitive forms of rackets made their appearance.

        PARKE CUMMINGS
        American Tennis

Lawn tennis began in America when Mary Ewing Outerbridge of Staten Island, NY returned from a Bermuda vacation in March of 1874 with an armful of crudely strung bats. These rackets were held in customs for they did not know the purpose of the rackets and what duty they had to charge on them.

PARKE CUMMINGS
American Tennis

———

The game is well enough for lazy or weak men, but men who have rowed or taken part in a nobler sport should blush to be seen playing lawn tennis.

Harper's Weekly (September 1878)

The tennis balls used prior to the advent of the modern game were made of wool and wrapped in leather. They lacked much bounce and were very heavy. The French King Charles VIII died after being hit on the head by one.

RICHARD EVANS
Encyclopedia of World Tennis

Naming Roland Garros, the French Open's Parisian facility, after one of the country's most coveted World War I heroes, honored the French fighter pilot and the hope that the tennis to unfold would follow in gallant tradition.

ANDREA LEAND
Tennis Week (June 20, 2001)

This is a permanent tribute to the man who had the vision to transform Roland Garros from an important tournament to one of the greatest grand slams—and the greatest tournament on clay in the tennis calendar.

FRANCISCO RICCI BITTI, FORMER ITF PRESIDENT, ON RENAMING COURT CENTRALE "COURT PHILIPPE CHATRIER"
ITF newsletter (May 29, 2001)

I will always regard him as the father of international tennis. He worked tirelessly toward the creation of Open tennis in 1968 in which professionals and amateurs play together and he was the indomitable force in returning tennis to the Olympics.

FRANCISCO RICCI BITTI, FORMER ITF PRESIDENT, ON PHILIPPE CHATRIER
The New York Times (June 24, 2000)

We have always valued our participation in international sport because we believe it to be a great opportunity for promotion of better international understanding and because it contained no distinction of race, class or creed. We view, with great misgivings, any action which may well undermine all that is valuable in international competitiveness.

The Story of the Davis Cup, by Alan Trengove, quoting Fred Perry and Bunny Austin's letter to the *London Times* in 1933 after non-Aryans were barred from representing Germany in sports

THE QUOTABLE TENNIS PLAYER

Connors gave tennis some publicity and the U.S. Open a boost—I thank him for that—but fifty years from now when you look at the record book you will see my name as the winner—the attention on Jimmy took the pressure off me—I sort of sneaked in the back way, as usual.

STEFAN EDBERG, FORMER U.S. OPEN AND WIMBLEDON CHAMPION
Fort Lauderdale Sun-Sentinel (September 9, 1991)

It is immensely significant that Judy Levering will be the first woman president. It is the right thing to do. The time is overdue and it shows the world that men and women are equally important to the game.

HARRY MARMION, FORMER USTA PRESIDENT
Fort Lauderdale Sun-Sentinel (August 23, 1998)

Tournament is a word derived from the old French word *tournier*, to turn around. Court tennis took over the language of chivalry, and a tournament became an elimination to determine the champion of anything.

ROBERT MINTON
Forest Hills: An Illustrated History

———

Such abusive language and gestures, abuse of racquet and balls and courtside excessiveness should not be tolerated. There should be a code of conduct requiring each player to agree to conduct himself in a manner which reflects well on his team and his country.

HENRY MERLO, president of Louisiana Pacific Corporation, the sponsor of the U.S. team, on the establishment of the code of conduct after Connors's and McEnroe's poor behavior at the 1984 Davis Cup

The Story of the Davis Cup, by Alan Trengove

In 1973, Margaret Court's $25,000 winner's check matched John Newcombe's prize, making it the first time men's and women's champions were paid equally in a major championship.

SUSAN B. ADAMS
The New York Times (August 30, 1998)

I felt very much at home here. From my first years on I felt I was one of them, and they made me feel like it. You can talk of the relationship we had. I felt they knew how to treat me and I was always trying to give them the best I've got.

BORIS BECKER, ON WIMBLEDON
The New York Times (July 4, 1997)

Becker was to Wimbledon what Jimmy Connors was to the U.S. Open, what Stan Musial, Wayne Gretsky and Magic Johnson were. The visiting athlete who transcends hometown jingleism. Becker even transcended nationalism.

GEORGE VECSEY
The New York Times (July 4, 1997)

We never had a streaker on Centre Court before, so I suppose it was inevitable eventually. Whilst we do not wish to condone the practice, it did provide some light amusement for our loyal fans.

WIMBLEDON OFFICIAL
The New York Times (July 8, 1996)

Every young WTA player should go to Billie Jean King and shake her hand because she single-handedly made it possible for the money that they are making today.

CHRIS EVERT
*Bravo Biography: Billie Jean King (*March 4, 2002)

Allison Danzig coined the phrase "grand slam" to hail the rarely turned trick of winning the four major championships within a calendar year in 1933.

BUD COLLINS
My Life with the Pros

The French covered our expenses; not the USTA. We had to pay for our rooms and meals. We never got a dime. The first year I got to the finals in 1946 I had to pay for tickets so my parents could come and watch.

DORIS HART, WINNER OF SINGLES, DOUBLES, AND MIXED DOUBLES AT ALL THE GRAND SLAMS, ON THE EARLY DAYS OF THE U.S. OPEN
Tennis Week (April 2, 2002)

She deserves tribute for her contribution to women's pro tennis because she did a great job of organizing and promoting the women's circuit in the difficult early years. Without her, women's tennis would still be in the dark ages.

MARGARET SMITH COURT, FORMER WTA PLAYER, ON GLADYS HELDMAN
Court on Court

It is difficult to overestimate the impact Gladys Heldman had on the growth and development of tennis. She signed nine women for a token one dollar to start the women's pro tour.

RICHARD EVANS
Encyclopedia of World Tennis

I was thinking back to the time when I signed that first contract for one dollar, back then we used to talk about things like this. We used to talk about how tennis would be prime-time. How we would embrace people over a wide spectrum. This night transcends tennis.

BILLIE JEAN KING, commenting on the first U.S. Open final on prime-time TV (2001)

Judging from the interest, it was a phenomenal event. It really transcends sports when it became a news item. People who wouldn't usually watch tennis would tune in to watch what the news was about.

SEAN McMANUS, CBS SPORTS PRESIDENT, ON THE FIRST PRIME-TIME WOMEN'S FINAL

Except for something like the U.S. Open, there will be a fall-off in the tournament attendance because of increased television coverage. The pros still have to start giving a little more, and not find fault with everything that's done for them.

BILL TALBERT, FORMER U.S. DAVIS CUP CAPTAIN, PREDICTING THE FUTURE OF TENNIS (1975)
The Tennis Bubble by Rich Koster

The jump in prize money we've had in the past five years won't be repeated. Tickets to tournaments may be harder to get as tennis becomes a fixture in sports.

LAMAR HUNT, FORMER TENNIS TOUR SPONSOR, PREDICTING THE FUTURE OF TENNIS (1975)
The Tennis Bubble by Rich Koster

———•··•———

There's no stopping the game because of the private enterprise that's concerned. The game would function better if it were under one hat, and I think we're headed that way, toward a tennis czar.

ROD LAVER, FORMER MEN'S TOUR PLAYER, PREDICTING THE FUTURE OF TENNIS (1975)
The Tennis Bubble by Rich Koster

Someday, there's going to be a $25,000 tournament.

BARRY MACKAY, FORMER MEN'S TOUR PLAYER, PREDICTING THE FUTURE
OF TENNIS (1975)
The Tennis Bubble by Rich Koster

I have been watching tennis and watching the best longer than most people here. This is not a boast, just the unfortunate accident of the calendar.

ALISTAIR COOKE, TENNIS HISTORIAN (1994)

You got this sport that used to be so lily white and you have two African-American women playing for the U.S. Open 2001 title in the Arthur Ashe Stadium and the stadium next door is the Louis Armstrong Stadium. That says it all. Arthur Ashe is smiling.

ED BRADLEY
CBS News (2001)

Bobby Riggs, the male chauvinist pig who set out to prove the inferiority of female athletes, was the man many now credit with making women's tennis and women's athletics as a whole the force they are today.

JOE GARNER
And the Crowd Goes Wild

It is over! The long-awaited match hustled and promoted ceaselessly and shrewdly by Bobby Riggs

HOWARD COSELL, ON THE BILLIE JEAN KING AND BOBBY RIGGS
MATCH
And the Crowd Goes Wild by Joe Garner

Everyone was carefully selected and trained. Being part of a professional sport was your meal ticket to a better life and you didn't want to worry about not making it. You just had to have great hopes for your future.

JENNIFER ANCHEVSKI, FORMER SOVIET PLAYER AND CURRENT COACH,
FROM THE AUSTRALIAN OPEN OFFICIAL PROGRAM 2002, ON RUSSIAN
TRAINING FACILITIES

Billie Jean King led the charge to open tennis, demanding that tennis players be paid as professionals instead of under the table.

ROBERT LIPSYTE, WRITER FOR *THE NEW YORK TIMES*
Bravo Biography: Billie Jean King (March 4, 2002)

If I ever was to write another book the title would be, *We Were Robbed*. I would go through history to show great players who, because of WWII or turning pro before the open era, were not able to compete at the slams.

JACK KRAMER
Tennis Week (June 26, 2001)

We could have named it USTA Stadium or we could have named it after a person. . . . Arthur was a champion who transcended the sport. We were lucky to have Arthur.

JUDY LEVERING, USTA PRESIDENT, ON NAMING THE NEW U.S. OPEN
COURT "ARTHUR ASHE STADIUM"
The New York Times (August 29, 1999)

In 1938, at age ten, Bill Talbert contracted diabetes at a time when this meant you basically shut down and did nothing physical. He asked his doctor if he could try a sport [and was told], "If you want to gamble with your life and health you might try tennis," thinking that shouldn't tax him unduly. . . . He went on to become one of America's greatest players ever.

HOWARD COSELL
Fort Lauderdale Sun-Sentinel (June 24, 1988)

Training and Preparation

The idea of training hard doesn't work. Training right works.

STEVE STEFANKI, FORMER U.S. JUNIOR DAVIS CUP COACH
Inside Tennis (October 2001)

———•••———

There is a very fine line between undertraining and overtraining, and the spot right between those two extremes is peak form.

CHRIS EVERT
Tennis (October 2001)

Before a match I go back to the locker room and I visualize my opponent's strokes, his strengths and his weaknesses. It gives me a better understanding of my game and makes me a better student of the game.

LEANDER PAES, ATP PLAYER
Inside Tennis (December 2001)

Try to find a mix of stronger and weaker practice partners. Against the weaker player you can work on your weaknesses and against the stronger players you have to use your strengths.

FRED STOLLE, FORMER MEN'S TOUR PLAYER
The Tennis Lover's Book of Wisdom edited by Criswell Freeman

My talent was for hard work.

> IVAN LENDL
> *Tennis Week* (June 24, 2001)

———

You have to learn to live on the road, train on the road and not get injured on the road.

> ALEXANDRA STEVENSON, WTA PLAYER, ON THE LIFE OF A PRO (2001)

———

I've been working very hard for years. I didn't win this match today. I won it in practice.

> ALEX CORRETJA, ATP PLAYER, ON ROLAND GARROS 2001

You have to be strong enough to stand the pressure. You don't only have to be better than your opponents, you must stay better.

ANDREI MEDVEDEV, ATP PLAYER, AT ROLAND GARROS 1999

Tennis has changed to a fitness and strength sport. You have no chance without physical and mental fitness. You have to be focused on your aims and work very hard.

ANDREI MEDVEDEV, ATP PLAYER (1999)

The cost of producing even a journeyman player on the circuit is unbelievable. You can't justify it in any way. It's a black hole. I tell parents, "If you are hoping for a return on your investment, you are dead wrong."

JIM LOEHR, SPORTS PSYCHOLOGIST
Ladies of the Court by Michael Mewshaw

... the model by which tennis parents should be measured. Although conservative in theory, their flexible support system provided five children room to grow as individuals.

NEIL AMDUR, ON COLETTE AND JIMMY EVERT
World Tennis (December 1989)

It reminds me of my childhood where we would hit in a parking lot and use a string between the cars for a net. It goes to show you don't need the best conditions, if you have dedication you can make it.

MONICA SELES, ON STREET CLINICS (2001)

Out in sparsely populated areas of Australia the family tennis court was a refuge from the meager conditions. There was nothing to do but watch animals and screw around. So fathers built courts to keep their children from screwing around too much.

FRED STOLLE, FORMER MEN'S TOUR PLAYER
Remembrance of Games Past by John Sharnik

It doesn't matter if you have a coach, a psychologist, a trainer, a masseuse, a stringer, you know, it's about what you do on the court.

TIM HENMAN, ATP PLAYER, AT WIMBLEDON 2001

I was once too lazy to give the kind of commitment it takes to be a champion. I was trying to find the easy way. I know now.

MARK PHILIPPOUSSIS, ATP PLAYER
Fort Lauderdale Sun-Sentinel (December 1, 2001)

Even a small injury and you're out. These days any-body can beat you if you can't get your practice time in due to injury.

MARTINA HINGIS
Palm Springs Desert Sun (March 10, 2002)

I've probably taken more private lessons than any human being alive.

AARON KRICKSTEIN, FORMER TOP FIVE ATP PLAYER
Great Jews in Sports by Robert Slater

I played six great matches, but after that I had to learn to play the game. I really had no clue.

ALEXANDRA STEVENSON, WTA PLAYER (2001), TWO YEARS AFTER GETTING TO THE SEMIFINALS AT WIMBLEDON

In a sport where coaching egos are boundless, start with Bollettieri, move on to Braden and a dozen others; Paul Annacone exhibits no need to boast about how he has taken his player to number one. He's talkative but never loud. He is pensive but never at a loss for a thoughtful comment.

CHARLES BRINKER
Fort Lauderdale Sun-Sentinel (December 9, 2001)

I worked so hard that I was so physically fit that I was overfit and tired. But you have to experience it before you know what your body can take.

HANA MANDLIKOVA, FOUR-TIME GRAND SLAM CHAMPION
Fort Lauderdale Sun Sentinel (September 6, 1985)

No one ever said when I was growing up that I was ever going to be good or get to a grand slam final. I've proven a lot of people wrong. I'm not the most unbelievable athlete. I just tried so hard to get to where I am. I think it's great.

LINDSAY DAVENPORT
The New York Times (September 12, 1998)

Training the body to obey the mind as I have done differs from the more conventional method of getting the mind to obey the body.

CHRIS EVERT
Chrissie by Chris Evert and Neil Amdur

We had Martina Navratilova running in 107-degree heat in Texas and at 8,000 feet elevation in Aspen. The work may not show instantly, but in six months you will see the benefit.

NANCY LIEBERMAN, CONDITIONING COACH
Fort Lauderdale Sun-Sentinel (September 4, 1989)

All of our balls weren't good but if we had balls that were flat that was okay. It would just make them bend more to get to the shots and work harder.

ORACEN WILLIAMS, MOTHER OF THE WILLIAMS SISTERS, AT U.S. OPEN 2001

—•••—

I know now that I have to be the aggressor on the court. I can't just get the ball back and wait for it to happen. I have played one way all my life and it is hard to change that mentality.

MARY JO FERNANDEZ, FORMER TOP WTA PLAYER
Fort Lauderdale Sun-Sentinel (January 23, 1992)

—•••—

Sampras still thinks he can win every tournament. He has the mind of a champion. That does not turn off.

CLIFF DRYSDALE
ESPN (2002)

For the Love of the Game

I play for the love of the game. I think about having fun and what a pleasure playing tennis is. That seems to relax me and allow me to concentrate on playing my best.

EVONNE GOOLAGONG

The Tennis Lover's Book of Wisdom edited by Criswell Freeman

Every time I drive by the old house—I moved there when I was four—I always think about the tennis court there, between the house and the little store. It's not there anymore, of course, but to me it's still there. And I can envision me and my father playing.

PRESIDENT JIMMY CARTER
My Life with the Pros by Bud Collins

———

It was great. I wish I had thought of it.

ANDRE AGASSI, ON KUERTEN DRAWING A HEART ON THE COURT AT ROLAND GARROS (2001)

Everything that's ever happened to me in my life that's good has been because of tennis.

DODO CHENEY, FORMER NATIONAL CHAMPION
You Go Girl by Doren Kim and Charlie Jones

No sport other than tennis has been acclaimed from all disciplines as one that develops great benefits, physically, emotionally and mentally.

DR. JACK GROPPEL, SPORTS PERFORMANCE EXPERT
USTA Magazine (November 2001)

Regardless of your skill, if you are looking for a sport that provides all the benefits of interval training, tennis is one of the best. When you are stressed during a point, your heart rate goes up. In between the points your heart rate has a chance to come down.

DR. JACK GROPPEL, SPORTS PERFORMANCE EXPERT
The Corporate Athlete

One of tennis's alluring idiosyncrasies is being at once predictable and unpredictable. Even the experts in the press pit are challenged to choose champs from chumps consistently.

EUGENE L. SCOTT, EDITOR OF *TENNIS WEEK* MAGAZINE
Tennis Week (June 26, 2001)

There is no other sport like tennis. It's vigorous exercise that doesn't leave you destroyed and put you in an emergency room with a mid-life crisis.

Bradford Whitford, actor on the NBC series *The West Wing*
USTA Magazine (September 2001)

———

None of us chose tennis. Tennis chose us. One day you are the best player at your club. The next thing you know you are a tennis player—it becomes your whole life.

Yannick Noah
Hard Courts by John Feinstein

Tennis is a sport. No religion or caste is a barrier. Over the years I have never come across any barriers—religious or otherwise.

LEANDER PAES, ATP PLAYER
Inside Tennis (December 2001)

Just providing them with a feeling of self-worth, of being important and giving them hope is what matters. We all know tennis has a unique way of doing all that.

ART GOLDBLATT, ON THE NORWALK, CONNECTICUT GRASS ROOTS PROGRAM FOR CHILDREN
Tennis Week (November 22, 2001)

I am going to have a game of tennis. But what I really mean is, "I am going to have a wonderful time under the sky, in the sun . . . for a while for me the world will not exist."

HELEN WILLS MOODY, EIGHT-TIME WIMBLEDON CHAMPION
New York Tribune (October 25, 1938)

When I was a young kid I used to lie awake at night thinking about dying without anyone ever knowing I existed. I think now maybe people would know I lived.

HAROLD SOLOMON, FORMER ATP PLAYER
Great Jews in Sports by Robert Slater

Why I play my best matches against top players: I love the challenge.

KARINA HABSUDOVA, WTA PLAYER
WTA official Web site (www.wtatour.com)

It's the people you meet that makes it so enjoyable. And that has always been true.

FRANK PAPP, AGE 87, THE OLDEST SUPER SENIOR COMPETING, HAVING EARNED HIS WAY TO SECTIONALS 3.0
NCTA newsletter (November 2001)

Tennis is one of the good things in this world. Time on the court in the fresh air and sunshine is magnificent medicine. Sport, exhilaration, pressure and good exercise are all realized.

KITTY GODFREE, FORMER WOMEN'S TOUR PLAYER, AFTER WINNING
WIMBLEDON
The Illustrated Encyclopedia of World Tennis by John Haylett and Richard Evans

I like my job and think it is a wonderful thing being a tennis player.

VENUS WILLIAMS (2001)

I love to have an audience.

JULIA ABE, WTA PLAYER
WTA official Web site (www.wtatour.com)

People thought I was ruthless. I was. I didn't give a darn who was on the other side of the net. I'd knock you down if you got in the way. I just wanted to play my best.

ALTHEA GIBSON, FIVE-TIME GRAND SLAM CHAMPION
Breaking Barriers: A Houston Chronicle Special Report (July 1950)

This is definitely one of the toughest draws I've had anywhere, emotionally I looked at Pat Rafter and Andre Agassi as championship matches, but that is what I play for: the crowd, the atmosphere, walking out for the final, it's a rush. It's the reason I still play.

PETE SAMPRAS (2001)

The only possible regret I have is the feeling that I will die without having played enough tennis.

JEAN BOROTRA, FIVE-TIME GRAND SLAM CHAMPION
Remembrance of Games Past by John Sharnik

The actor on Broadway, the singer at La Scala, the dancer at the Bolshoi Theatre understand what the tennis player at Wimbledon feels. So does the golfer at the Masters, the football player in the Super Bowl, and the baseball player in the World Series. It isn't the money, the connoisseurs are here. We play for ourselves, and we perform and play because it's in us and we must.

Rod Laver
Tennis for the Bloody Fun of It by Rod Laver and Roy Emerson with Barry Tardhis

I am proud to be able to come back from everything that's happened in my life, and just to enjoy tennis and play this well. I think it shows everyone that it's never too late to realize your talent, or your dream.

Jennifer Capriati, on becoming ATP Female Athlete of the Year (2001)
Slamsports (December 27, 2001)

I'm tired of hearing that because you're thirty you're washed up. I still feel physically fine. I still love playing. I still have that deep down.

Pete Sampras
Palm Springs Desert Sun (April 4, 2002)

To be in the finals is why we play tennis. With all the fans in front of us, and broadcasted all over the world.

GUY FORGET, FRENCH DAVIS CUP COACH

www.daviscup.org

One of my doctors told me I wouldn't be playing at the pro level again after my knee operations. I want to prove him wrong.

MARK PHILIPOUSSIS, ATP PLAYER

Fort Lauderdale Sun-Sentinel (December 1, 2001)

Why I love tennis is the pureness of the competition. You are out there by yourself. There are no style points. No coaches, no judges.

MARTY DAVIS, FORMER ATP PLAYER AND CURRENT UNIVERSITY OF CALIFORNIA SANTA BARBARA TENNIS COACH

We don't play tennis or music for any other reason than to have fun and raise consciousness.

CARLOS SANTANA

Inside Tennis, Northern California Tennis Association 2002 Yearbook

In the hospital I watched Monica Seles play her first exhibition match back from her stabbing. She was nervous and happy. Happy to be doing what she loved most in the world. When I saw this and her interview about how she was just going to enjoy tennis, I thought to myself, no doctor that doesn't even know what the U.S. Open is will tell me that I can't return to playing the tour. I made a remarkable recovery in less than one year.

DEBRA GRAHAM, WTA PLAYER, ON RETURNING TO TENNIS IN 1995
AFTER SUFFERING A LIFE-THREATENING BLOOD CLOT

Lleyton Hewitt plays for the right reasons. He is about trophies and winning.

TOM ROSS, OCTAGON SPORTS AGENT
San Francisco Chronicle (February 24, 2002)

—•—

For me tennis was my passion and it became my job. And I enjoy it so much being on the court. That's the best part of the game, to be on the court and fight to win or lose.

JUSTINE HENIN, WTA PLAYER
Palm Springs Desert Sun (March 10, 2002)

I like the way so many things in tennis relate to baseball. Reaching for a volley is like reaching for a sinking line drive. Serving is like throwing. Returning serve is like getting ready to hit. Going back for a lob is like going back for a fly ball.

PAUL O'NEILL, FORMER NEW YORK YANKEES OUTFIELDER
USTA Magazine (March 2, 2002)

People say I missed out on my childhood, but I don't think so. I had a great time playing tennis, winning matches and doing the things I love.

ANNA KOURNIKOVA
Anna Kournikova by Amanda Mawrence

Just to grab a racket, to run out on the court, to be with friends and crunch my less-than-awesome top-spin crosscourt backhand was an affirmative, an odd renewal. The modest celebration of the mundane conveyed the message—simple and therapeutic—the human spirit endures. It's going to be okay.

WILLIAM C. SIMONS, EDITOR OF *INSIDE TENNIS*, ON THE FIRST DAYS AFTER 9/11
Inside Tennis (October 2001)

Tennis is a game of sensations. The first sensation is effort, without which you never get into the other feelings. Tennis is played and watched for its sensations and the major final sensation, the outcome, often feels like love.

ELIOT BERRY
Tough Draw

Old tennis players don't fade away. They keep appearing at Forest Hills and stay close to the game. Like circus performers who claim to have sawdust in their veins, tennis players find it impossible to tear themselves away from the game.

MARTY BELL
Carnival at Forest Hills

We got the real sports fan into the game. I wanted the fan sitting there who worked his tail off to make his money and paid for his ticket because he wanted to be there.

JIMMY CONNORS, ABOUT HIS MATCHES WITH JOHN MCENROE
The New York Times (August 11, 1996)

It's a great bridge between different religions and cultures, people from different nationalities and walks of life.

LEANDER PAES, ATP PLAYER
Inside Tennis

I would rather play beautiful tennis than win. In fact when I am hitting and really playing, I can lose track of the purpose of it all.

VIRGINIA WADE, WIMBLEDON CHAMPION
Carnival at Forest Hills by Marty Bell

The State of the Game

Tennis is a game, but a game is a contest and a struggle. Fun and exciting to watch, it is a deadly serious encounter to the players. It means everything to them at the time.

ROBERT MINTON
Forest Hills: An Illustrated History

A doubles pairing is probably tougher than a marriage. You spend more time with your partner, practicing, playing, eating, hanging out than you do with your wife on most weeks.

PAT GALBRAITH, ATP PLAYER
International Tennis Magazine (January 1996)

Tennis is show business and you have to create excitement.

BILL TALBERT, FORMER DAVIS CUP COACH
Fort Lauderdale Sun-Sentinel (August 27, 1987)

———

Like art, tennis has the capacity to stop your heart and leave the incredible memory of a moment in which a human flew.

ROBERT LIPSYTE
The New York Times (September 8, 1991)

Magazine advertising is very expensive. A single page can cost tens of thousands of dollars. But with Vilas and Evert we get front page for our product. You can't buy the front page at any price.

GABRIELLA BRUSTEAGHI, HEAD OF ELLESSE SPORTS
Short Circuit by Michael Mewshaw

Aesthetics and charm are winning out over sports performance on the WTA tour. What do you think tennis is? The casting ground for the next James Bond movie?

NATALIE TAUZIAT
Les Dessous du Tennis Feminin

This is the toughest sport of them all. Other sports don't play every night, and when you are tired or hurt you don't get a substitute.

PANCHO GONZALEZ, TOP MEN'S PRO IN THE 1950S
Sport magazine (1988)

———•••———

Tennis pros are all accompanied by a bizarre retinue who helps them live spectacularly embroidered private lives that exceed the saga of my ordinary nineteenth-century Russian model.

FRANK DEFORD
The Best of Frank Deford

Tennis players love to boast how easy it is to play the game quickly. I skipped lunch with Howie yesterday and we played two sets but were back in time for the budget session.

FRANK DEFORD
The Best of Frank Deford

I've never met a great tennis player who ever made fun of the way somebody else hit the ball.

ROY EMERSON, FORMER MEN'S TOUR PLAYER
The Tennis Lover's Book of Wisdom edited by Criswell Freeman

Tennis players manage to look bad in tennis clothes because they stick the extra ball in their pockets or underwear and look lumpy.

FRANK DEFORD
The Best of Frank Deford

————

Tennis can be an amazingly becoming sport for human beings to play, or a spasm of swift and convulsive action.

CATHERINE BELL AND ROY PETERS
Passing Shots

This is an era of blast-away power; just kill the ball
until the opponent drops dead.

BRUCE JENKINS, 2001 U.S. OPEN

Tennis is a perfect combination of violent action taking place in an atmosphere of total tranquility.

BILLIE JEAN KING
The Tennis Lover's Book of Wisdom edited by Criswell Freeman

You can't measure success if you have never failed.

STEFFI GRAF
You Go Girl by Doren Kim and Charlie Jones

———

Tennis essentially remains a game of artistry and psychology between two individuals that must be won with the brain as well as with the body.

The Right Set: A Tennis Anthology edited by Caryl Phillips

We are not tennis players, we are stars.

ANNA KOURNIKOVA
Venus Envy by L. Jon Wertheim

Tournament tennis is a sport for selfish people because the game requires preoccupation with one's own performance, one's own state of mind.

CATHERINE BELL AND ROY PETERS
Passing Shots

With pro tennis combining a men's and women's event, one plus one equals more than two.

CHARLIE PASARELL, FORMER MEN'S TOUR PLAYER AND CURRENT DIRECTOR OF THE NEWSWEEK TOURNAMENT AND EVERT CUP

The game is getting faster as we are unfortunately slowing down.

LARRY DODGE, NATIONALLY RANKED SENIOR PLAYER (1995)

It is important to recognize that tennis can be a vehicle to numerous opportunities beyond the confines of the sport. Our committee believes strongly in the ability and responsibility of organized tennis to be a fulcrum for good works in the community.

LOU MAUNUPAU, CHAIRMAN OF THE NOR-CAL MINORITY PARTICIPATION COMMITTEE, 2001
Northern California Tennis Association Newsletter (November 2001)

I don't consider it pressure, I consider it an opportunity. The whole country is rooting for me.

ANDY RODDICK, ATP PLAYER, ON THE PRESSURE OF BEING THE NEXT GREAT AMERICAN PLAYER (MONTREAL 2001)
ESPN

I wish TV could figure out a way to capture the excitement that being at the event live presents.

PRESIDENT BILL CLINTON, ROLAND GARROS 2001

Tennis is a great game, not in need of new rules or balls that weigh more and kill the players' arms. It just needs to be promoted better.

RICHARD EVANS
Tennis Week (July 2001)

I don't believe the game itself [is] too fast . . . Why slow it down? The bigger ball and slower court is silly.

JAN MICHAEL GAMBILL, ATP PLAYER
Tennis (August 2001)

Despite all the hoopla about how much power is in the game and how big physically everyone is, the reality is that in 2001 the number one player, Lleyton Hewitt, is only five-ten.

MARTY DAVIS, FORMER ATP PLAYER

He shed light on tennis by making it palatable to television.

BUD COLLINS, ON JIMMY VAN ALLEN, THE INVENTOR OF THE TIEBREAKER
My Life with the Pros

Matches lasted too long. It struck me that there had to be a better, more exciting way to control the length of matches.

> JIMMY VAN ALLEN, ON INVENTING THE TIEBREAKER
> *My Life with the Pros* by Bud Collins

Money is killing tennis. The motivation for true greatness is gone for most players by the time they are eighteen. Connors says when he started you had to win to get rich.

> PHILIPPE CHATRIER, FORMER ITF PRESIDENT
> *Hard Courts* by John Feinstein

An inferior player on occasion can beat the superior player by raising the level of play. The players call it playing out of your tree, the shots just come like manna from heaven.

NEIL AMDUR
A Long Way, Baby by Grace Lichtenstein

You must play tennis the same way you live your life. You can make mistakes, you can miss; but you can't play brilliant one minute and dumb the next. You must be consistently smart.

KAREN WOODELL, NORTHERN CALIFORNIA TENNIS LEAGUE MANAGER

Tennis is a great competition, it has a great care spirit. There is a level of style, sophistication, humor and competitiveness that serves us well.

KEVIN WUOFF, NIKE EXECUTIVE AND INCOMING CEO OF THE WTA
Tennis Week (November 2001)

We competed hard, but we enjoyed it more. We used to meet people and we would go to their homes. Now the players don't seem to have much social contact with the world. They practice, play the match and go back to the hotel.

RAMANATHAN KRISHNAN, FORMER PLAYER
Remembrance of Games Past by John Sharnik

On tour there are a lot more good players than there were ten years ago. This is due to the popularity of tennis, particularly in Europe and in other parts of the world. And because of the financial rewards the pool of players gets deeper year in and year out.

BRAD STINE, PRO COACH
USPTA Magazine (December 2001)

The business of tennis is unique. Your assets are people, not sneakers or buildings or other objects. Those assets are young, sometimes rebellious and not highly educated. They often come with senior advisors and they depreciate quickly.

PHIL DE PICCIOTTO, PRESIDENT OF ATHLETIC REPRESENTATION AT OCTAGON (2001)

I feel the fans deserved to get involved, but if they called me a jerk I went back at them. It's the way I was brought up. It was surprising when I went to London and they took it so bad.

JOHN MCENROE
The New York Times (August 4, 1996)

Why doesn't the pro game go back to wood racquets? Then we would see the best tennis to be played. The athletes are better but it's incredible how much worse the game is technically.

JOHN MCENROE
The New York Times (August 4, 1996)

It's what you dream about, and my dream almost came true at this tournament. It's great when you come into a tournament with everyone in the world and you are still standing on the final day.

MALIVAI WASHINGTON, ESPN COMMENTATOR, ON HIS APPEARANCE AT THE 1996 WIMBLEDON FINAL
The New York Times (July 8, 1996)

In tennis you don't have to jump high, you don't have to be lightning quick. You can have different strengths that can make you a good tennis player.

LINDSAY DAVENPORT
The New York Times (September 12, 1998)

———

The first one in 1991 had the feeling of Woodstock the rock festival. This one in 1997 had the feeling of V-E Day at the Piccadilly Circus in 1945 and the England World Cup victory at Wembley in 1966.

GEORGE VECSEY, ON PEOPLE'S SUNDAY AT WIMBLEDON, WHEN DUE TO RAIN THE TOURNAMENT IS EXTENDED AND ALL TICKETS ARE SOLD ON THAT DAY
The New York Times (June 30, 1997)

The money in tennis has gotten so good that many top players can afford to retire upon the first squeaks and complaints from their bodies and their minds. When a tennis player can't be one or two they tend to retire abruptly and that is sad more for us than them.

GEORGE VECSEY
The New York Times (August 27, 1997)

Maybe you are not quite at the top, but you can be as good as ever at least until age thirty-three, if you want to pay the price off the court.

JACK KRAMER, ON THE HOPE THAT TOP GUYS STAY IN THE GAME
LONGER
Tennis Week (June 26, 2001)

Hard courts make the match more interesting for the fans because everyone can have a chance. They can serve and volley or stay back. But hard courts are difficult and tough on the body.

YANNICK NOAH
Fort Lauderdale Sun-Sentinel (September 4, 1988)

You have to earn the fans and you don't earn them overnight. You win their support by working hard and giving your best.

IVAN LENDL
Fort Lauderdale Sun-Sentinel (August 31, 1986)

American tennis continues as a stage conducting the eternal search for the noisy celebrity showdown. The ability to communicate with the crowd is a wonderful thing but the definition of personality is more than bouncing racquets off the court and throwing wristbands to the crowd.

HARVEY ARATON
The New York Times (August 29, 1996)

I love this program because it teaches kids more than tennis. We are using tennis as a vehicle to instill discipline, confidence and independent thinking—and we are succeeding

TONY BROCK, DIRECTOR OF THE SAFE PASSAGE TENNIS PROGRAM IN
SOUTHERN CALIFORNIA
Tennis Week (April 2, 2002)

As long as your mind wants to do it and your body holds up, there is no such thing as not being able to play on tour at thirty or thirty-two years old. The interest may go away and sometimes the willingness to make changes goes.

JOSE HIGUERAS
Inside Tennis (April 2, 2002)

The day you start giving priority to bogus ethics over human reaction you become a loser. Human reactions are priceless. Rules should never supersede to stifle emotions. Tennis is a very human game facing a danger that it will be strangled by unnecessary inhuman rules.

TED TINLING, TENNIS HISTORIAN
Fort Lauderdale Sun-Sentinel (May 27, 1990)

To produce tennis balls worthy of meeting the USTA or ITF specifications, generally sixteen manufacturing operations are involved.

United States Lawn Tennis Association Official Encyclopedia of Tennis (1972)

Hingis in 2001 goes into verbal wars with her opponents almost on purpose as if she knows that winning a grand slam might be beyond her, but staying in the spotlight must be done at any cost.

DIANE PUCIN
Los Angeles Times (September 7, 2001)

The beauty of that time of tennis was that each individual was a certain game and Tilden's greatest capacity was at adapting. These players today all do the same things against each other—Bill would have adapted and killed them all.

MANUEL ALONSO
Big Bill Tilden by Frank Deford

Tennis fathers have proliferated because unlike almost any other industry, tennis is free of sticky child labor laws. Many fathers stop working as soon as it becomes clear that his child has a better chance of bringing home the bacon.

PETER BODO
Courts of Babylon

I play big points in big matches pretty well—that's what the top ten guys do. That's the main focus of the sport.

WAYNE ARTHURS, ROLAND GARROS 2001

Living on the road sounds great. People think we are out partying all the time, drinking and chasing girls. What they don't know is mostly you're just in your hotel room alone.

MEL PURCELL
Short Circuit by Michael Mewshaw

Humor On and Off the Court

Good shot, bad luck and hell are the five basic words to be used in a game of tennis, though these, of course, can be slightly amplified.

VIRGINIA GRAHAM
The Quotable Woman by Elaine T. Partnow

When I was forty years old my doctor advised me that a man in his forties shouldn't be playing tennis. I heeded his advice carefully and could hardly wait until I reached fifty to start again.

SUPREME COURT JUSTICE HUGO BLACK
Treasury of Modern Quotations (February 1963)

Writing free verse is like playing tennis with the net down.

ROBERT FROST (1935)
Oxford Dictionary of Humorous Quotations

———

The score was 20–20 in a match against Lew Hoad and I did the splits going for a shot. Snap! I felt something go. A tendon? No—my jockstrap.

ROD LAVER, ON THE LONGEST SET HE EVER PLAYED
Tennis for the Bloody Fun of It by Rod Laver and Roy Emerson with Barry Tardis

We are merely the stars' tennis-balls, struck
    and banded
Which way please them.

> JOHN WEBSTER, BRITISH DRAMATIST (1580–1625)
> *The Duchess of Malfi,* Act V, Scene IV

I bend down because I can.

> KEN BEERS, FORMER MEN'S NATIONAL CHAMPION, AT AGE 92, WHEN
> ASKED WHY HE BENDS DOWN TO PICK UP THE BALL INSTEAD OF TAP-
> PING IT UP (2001)

"Baseball is 90 percent mental and the other half physical." The same is true of tennis, only more so.

CRISWELL FREEMAN, QUOTING YOGI BERRA
The Tennis Lover's Book of Wisdom

———

There is only one person whose talents you can appreciate completely and whose lapses you can tolerate easily and forgive instantly. . . . Unfortunately you cannot be your own partner, so you'll just have to resign yourself to settling for second best.

BILLIE JEAN KING AND FRED STOLLE
How to Play Mixed Doubles

A method of playing tennis in which the natural antipathy between the different sides of the nets is furthered by the mutual antagonism on each side of the nets.

LANCE TINGAY, BRITISH TENNIS WRITER (1915–1990), WHEN ASKED FOR A DEFINITION OF DOUBLES
How to Play Mixed Doubles by Billie Jean King and Fred Stolle

No one is more sensitive about his game than a weekend tennis player.

JIMMY CANNON
The Oxford Dictionary Of Humorous Quotations

You can't buy groceries with glory. Why don't you turn professional now and cash in? It's your great chance, why not grab it?

HARPO MARX, TO FRED PERRY, ON TURNING PRO IN 1934
The Right Set: A Tennis Anthology by Caryl Phillips (editor)

—◆◆◆—

Some people get so all they want out of life is food, sex, clothes and a well-strung tennis racquet.

ALLIE RITZENBERG, PROFESSIONAL TENNIS INSTRUCTOR
Reader's Digest (August 1973)

I discovered tennis in 1968. Since then I play whenever I can. Tennis is very useful. Every time I play I lose two pounds. You won't find that on the golf course.

ENGELBERT HUMPERDINCK
Tennis (March 2002)

The shot they were commenting on was so bad it drove Martina Navratilova into speaking Yiddish.

MARY CARILLO, HBO COMMENTATOR, WIMBLEDON 2001

Sorry, mate.

PATRICK RAFTER, ATP PLAYER, AFTER CATCHING A BAD TOSS WHILE SERVING IN A MATCH

Once Goran said God was on his side at Wimbledon—
I was done.

TIM HENMAN, ATP PLAYER (2001)

Don't worry. The opponents will get tired of winning pretty soon.

SAID BY NAOMI BIGLIARDI'S PARTNER IN A USTA 4.0 MATCH THEY WERE LOSING

———•••———

That Gullikson is a great player. Last week he beat me playing left handed. This week he beats me playing right handed.

A YOUNG EUROPEAN PLAYER WHO LOST BACK-TO-BACK WEEKS TO THE GULLIKSON TWINS, THINKING THEY WERE ONE PERSON

[Mal Washington and Richard Krajicek] lined up for the traditional protocol at the net before play began on Centre Court—but all eyes were suddenly elsewhere. A female streaker burst onto the scene and broke the tension as both players shared a laugh at a highly surreal moment. Those fleeting seconds were the most requested piece of video transmission in the BBC compound that year.

SUE BARKER
BBC (1996)

I lost because the draw was fixed.

JELENA DOKIC, WTA PLAYER, 2001 AUSTRALIAN OPEN

There are three Gorans—good, bad and emergency Goran, who he calls the mediator—who mollifies his split personalities. He is here. He always has to be here.

GORAN IVANISEVIC, ATP PLAYER, AT THE 2001 U.S. OPEN

I have never seen anyone spin the racquet in his hand after every shot except Juan Carlos Ferrero.

LUKE JENSEN (2001)
ESPN

Goran Ivanisevic, playing in Brighton 2000, broke or destroyed the only three racquets he brought with him and had to default.

RICHARD EVANS
Tennis Week (July 2001)

With Roy Emerson we had a rule. We either go to bed at a reasonable hour or stay out all night. On bigger tournaments one of us would go back to the hotel and get enough sleep for both of us.

FRED STOLLE
My Life with the Pros, by Bud Collins

Norman can even lob from the missionary position.

STAN BEAINY, RETIRED BUSINESS EXECUTIVE AND TENNIS STUDENT (1997), IN RESPONSE TO ANOTHER STUDENT'S COMMENT ABOUT A GREAT AND FREQUENT LOBBER BEING CAPABLE OF LOBBING FROM ANY POSITION ON THE COURT

To the utter, howling derision of his mates, Rafter has made the lists of the Most Beautiful People in the World. "Nothing wrong with that," Rafter says, grinning beatifically. "But I've noticed you get better looking the more U.S. Opens you win and money you make."

PATRICK RAFTER, ATP PLAYER
GQ

My coach, Mats Wilander, thinks in Swedish. I think in Russian. We talk in English.

MARAT SAFIN, ATP PLAYER, 2001 U.S. OPEN

When I got up I didn't know where I was. I didn't know if it was Indianapolis, Barcelona or whatever.

ALEX CORRETJA, AFTER AGASSI'S OVERHEAD KNOCKED HIM DOWN (1988)

The serve was invented so the net can play.

BILL COSBY
The Tennis Lover's Book of Wisdom edited by Criswell Freeman

He is the Jerry Lewis of tennis. The French love him.

CRAIG KILBORN, ON ANDY RODDICK (2001)

Lob your message in. If it's over my head, I'll return it with an overhead smash.

TELEPHONE ANSWERING MACHINE MESSAGE OF DODO CHENEY,
OCTOGENARIAN WOMEN'S TENNIS LEGEND
You Go Girl by Kim Doren and Charlie Jones

Death is nature's way of giving someone else your tennis court.

JOHNNY CARSON
The Tennis Lover's Book of Wisdom edited by Criswell Freeman

Lew Hoad had concentration problems. Ken Rosewall said when they played doubles Hoad often became very engrossed in the match on the other court—to his present match's detriment.

PETER ROWLEY
Ken Rosewall: Twenty Years at the Top

Stefan Edberg is quiet even for a Swede.

MATS WILANDER, FELLOW SWEDE AND FORMER NUMBER ONE PLAYER
IN THE WORLD

You cannot be serious!

JOHN MCENROE, RESPONDING TO ALL THE LINESMEN WHO MADE
CALLS HE DIDN'T AGREE WITH

Why, it was the day in 1926 that Betty Nuthall's knickers fell down in Centre Court.

COLONEL JACKIE SMITH, TENNIS HISTORIAN AND MEMBER OF THE
WIMBLEDON ESTABLISHMENT, WHEN ASKED ABOUT THE MOST MEMO-
RABLE OCCASION OF HIS NUMEROUS WIMBLEDONS

Virginia Wade and Carole Rosser were playing in 1962 at Wimbledon and both were swearing like sailors. "What's that she's saying?" said one of two aged ladies, responding to the players' language with puzzled looks. The other replied, "I don't understand a word of it, my dear. I think they're Spanish."

BUD COLLINS
My Life with the Pros

The first two weeks I was there Aaron never said a word to me. I thought he didn't like me. It wasn't until later that I learned Aaron doesn't talk to anyone.

DAVID WHEATON, ATP PLAYER, ON ROOMING WITH AARON
KRICKSTEIN AT BOLLETTIERI'S TENNIS ACADEMY
Hard Courts by John Feinstein

———

The best part of Natalie Tauziat's game today has been her screaming.

PAM SHRIVER, ESPN COMMENTATOR, AT THE 2001 SANEX
CHAMPIONSHIPS

The guy plays unbelievable tennis all the time—either unbelievable good or unbelievable bad.

ANDRE CHESNOKOV, FORMER ATP PLAYER, REFERRING TO HENRI LECONTE
Hard Courts by John Feinstein

There is a big trophy but they don't give you that. They give you a replica. I asked for the big one but they said, "No, we only put your name on it."

ARANTXA SANCHEZ VICARIO, WTA PLAYER, 1994 U.S. OPEN

"A bit too ambitious on that forehand."

"Oh, I say, that was a glorious shot."

"McEnroe's throw up has been off." [referring to a toss]

"Boris has astonished the crowd with his enormous length." [on missing long]

> MICHAEL MEWSHAW, ON BBC COMMENTARY BEING AS ANNOYING AS
> U.S. COMMENTARY
> *Short Circuit*

Larry's only shortcoming in life, as far as I know, has been his failure to solidify my backhand. (Larry has also failed to climb Mt. Everest, and I put both failures in the same category!)

BARRY TARDHIS, ON LARRY JESTICE
Tennis for the Bloody Fun of It by Rod Laver and Roy Emerson with Barry Tardhis

The only thing that scares me about Noah is his hair.

JOHN MCENROE, ON PLAYING YANNICK NOAH WHEN NOAH WORE DREDLOCKS
Days of Grace: A Memoir by Arthur Ashe

She was described as having tennis elbow of the personality.

L. JON WERTHEIM, ON GABRIELA SABATINI
Venus Envy

At the Italian Open the matches were three out of five sets. At the end of the second set a famous coach ran down to the court to help carry his player's equipment off the court. As the coach successfully gathered the equipment and left the court, the player had to chase him down to inform him the match was not over and the player was in further need of his equipment.

MARTY DAVIS, FORMER ATP PLAYER

He was having a blinder.

JOHN FITZGERALD, AUSTRALIAN DAVIS CUP CAPTAIN 2001, ON
NICOLAS ESCUDE'S GREAT PLAY IN THE DAVIS CUP FINAL (2001)
www.daviscup.org

Compared to other sports . . . I wasn't getting paid
enough.

YEVGENY KAFELNIKOV, ATP PLAYER (2001)

Boy, have I been losing to some lousy tennis players lately.

OPPONENT OF JEFF UNGER, FORMER UNIVERSITY OF WISCONSIN TEN-
NIS PLAYER, AFTER JEFF HAD WON THE MATCH

When I start to lose to players like him I've got to reconsider what I am doing even playing this game.

JOHN MCENROE, AFTER A 1995 LOSS TO BRAD GILBERT
Agassi & Ecstacy by Paul Bauman

I used to be the ball boy for Big Bill Tilden and helped
Don Budge with his serve.

David Letterman
The Late Show (February 6, 2002)

———•••———

Reading Bill Tilden's book. Didn't everyone?

John Newcomb, after winning Wimbledon in 1967, when asked
where he originally learned the game
Big Bill Tilden: The Triumphs and the Tragedy by Frank Deford

On the coin toss Martina said, "Do you want me to break your serve first or hold?" The umpire looked shocked. But we just both cracked up.

LINDSAY DAVENPORT, ON A MATCH SHE PLAYED WITH MARTINA HINGIS.
The New York Times (August 24, 1997)

As a kid I would hit against the wall emulating my favorite players and their styles. It didn't take me long to learn a simple lesson—the wall never lost.

CONCHITA MARTINEZ, WIMBLEDON CHAMPION
Venus Envy by L. Jon Wertheim

The nicest way to tell you that your shot missed: "The net robbed you."

TIM GULLIKSON, FORMER ATP PLAYER

I never misbehaved because I was afraid if I did anything like that my father could come up and kick my ass.

ARTHUR ASHE
Days of Grace: A Memoir

Aging tennis players are not miraculously free of problems with their wheels . . . they lived with the same problems all their lives . . . age, in the player's view, is something that happens to your game, and only incidentally to your body.

JOHN SHARNIK
Remembrance of Games Past

I was playing mixed doubles in the World Team League. I told my top-ranked female partner that I would poach on her first serve and she should hit it to the opponent's backhand. She responded that she normally doesn't aim her serve, but if I liked she would try.

MARTY DAVIS, FORMER ATP PLAYER

The Tournaments

Crowds at Wimbledon miss nothing and are polite. At the U.S. Open they like drama and emotion. At Foro Italico they throw cushions. The British do not approve of such things. When a player misbehaves they cry shame.

JOHN MCPHEE
"Centre Court," *Playboy* (June 1971)

The atmosphere at Wimbledon is unbelievable to play in. It's something that when I first saw it as a five-year-old I knew I wanted to be involved in that.

TIM HENMAN, ATP PLAYER (2001)

It's what the atmosphere instills here, things come to a pitch. The best grass, best crowd. The loyalty you feel, the whole thing is important and you play your best tennis.

ROD LAVER, FORMER MEN'S TOUR PLAYER, ON WIMBLEDON
"Centre Court," by John McPhee, *Playboy* (June 1971)

Wimbledon is the nursery of the game. It breeds the giants of the past. Players who by the exercise of their art, the vigor of their physique and the force of their personalities inspired countries beyond to accept and play the cult of tennis.

> A. WALLIS MYERS, FORMER MEN'S TOUR PLAYER
> *The Right Set* by Caryl Phillips, editor

This is the granddaddy of them all. When you step out onto the court, the whole world is watching. I feel connected to this place. It feels like a cathedral.

> PETE SAMPRAS, ON WIMBLEDON
> *The New York Times* (June 20, 1999)

I hate the city, the environment and the facility. There is noise, and the people in the stands are never quiet. They should drop a bomb on the place.

KEVIN CURREN, FORMER ATP PLAYER, AFTER FIRST-ROUND LOSS AT THE U.S. OPEN (1985)

Decorum is checked at the door. The crowd is loud, it heckles. It sides with a player. They want to see some blood spilled. The spectators are an amalgam of knowledgeable, ignorant, crude, rude and reserved.

H. A. BRANHAM, ON THE U.S. OPEN CROWD
Sampras: A Legend in the Works by H. A. Branham

I've been through everything at the Open. That's where it all began for me. It's the place where I've won, where I've been injured, where I've been sick and where I've had great matches.

PETE SAMPRAS (2001)

If you can meet with triumph and disaster and treat those two imposters just the same.

EXCERPT FROM RUDYARD KIPLING'S POEM *If*, INSCRIBED ON THE ENTRANCE TO WIMBLEDON CENTRE COURT

The thing is that you are not necessarily playing for your country when you play Davis Cup. You are playing for the USTA—a few selfish people. I play for my country every time I step on the court. I am Billie Jean King of the United States.

BILLIE JEAN KING
The Tennis Bubble by Rich Koster

This is a bona fide global competition that has been going on for 102 years with more nations in the ITF, which governs the Davis Cup, than there are in the United Nations.

GENE SCOTT, EDITOR OF *TENNIS WEEK*, ON THE DAVIS CUP
Tennis Week (November 27, 2001)

It's not just for yourself. People are depending on you. The umpire does not say, "Game Gonzalez." He says, "Game United States."

PANCHO GONZALEZ, ON THE DAVIS CUP
The Story of the Davis Cup by Alan Trengove

———

The fans at the U.S. Open like a champion with a heart. They like a guy who can win in the fifth set, especially coming from behind.

JIM SARNI
Fort Lauderdale Sun-Sentinel (September 9, 1991)

The U.S. Open epitomizes the hustle, bustle and hoopla of New York. There are so many things that are out of your control you must learn to adapt. One day the place is a ninety-nine-degree cement jungle, the next day there could be a hurricane.

PAUL ANNACONE
The New York Times (August 30, 1997)

At the U.S. Open there is no coddling audience, just atmosphere. Either go with the flow and let the Open electrify you or expect to get electrocuted by it.

ROBIN FINN
The New York Times (August 30, 1999)

I look at the U.S. Open as a typical New Yorker. It's loud, it's confident, it's a bit cocky and it likes a challenge. It keeps you concentrated.

MARTINA HINGIS
The New York Times (August 30, 1999)

I have a little trophy case at home I've got to fill up. . . Once you win [at Wimbledon], it's pretty addictive.

VENUS WILLIAMS (2001)

The feeling among the top players is that Wimbledon is the pinnacle and the All-England Lawn Tennis Club is the palace guarding the history, the drama, the triumphs and the tragedies of the game.

BARBARA POTTER, FORMER WTA PLAYER
The New York Times (July 7, 1996)

The Players

The most important player ever in tennis history was Billie Jean King with her mixture of feminism, general gifts of leadership and athletic brilliance.

ARTHUR ASHE
Days of Grace: A Memoir

If I had a shot I could hit down his throat, I did. And then I'd say, "See, Jimmy, even your mother will do that to you."

GLORIA THOMPSON CONNORS, MOTHER OF JIMMY CONNORS
You Go Girl by Kim Doren and Charlie Jones

I have not the genius of Tilden nor the physical qualities of Borotra or of a Cochet. If I have sometimes succeeded in beating them it is because I have willed with all my force to win, to utilize the means which were within my reach.

RENE LACOSTE, SEVEN-TIME GRAND SLAM CHAMPION (1927)
Tough Draw by Eliot Berry

Arthur was an ambassador of what was right. An ambassador of dignity and class.

BRYANT GUMBLE
Arthur Ashe, Citizen of the World, HBO sports documentary
(1994)

A stately redwood whose powering presence binds us to the glories of the past, the power of the present and the potential of the future.

NEIL AMDUR, ON TED TINLING
World Tennis (December 1989)

McEnroe wanted to impose his will on everyone. Not content to play his opponent, he insisted on calling lines, lecturing umpires, chastising spectators, vilifying journalists and choreographing courtside cameramen and photographers.

MICHAEL MEWSHAW
Short Circuit

Her legacy beyond the two-handed backhand is her dignity. Chris always handled herself with class on the court. She did the most with what she had. If there was a way to win she found it.

MARTINA NAVRATILOVA, ON CHRIS EVERT
Sports Illustrated (August 28, 1989)

I would like to be remembered as someone who, even through trials and tribulations, can be an inspiration to other people who are also down and out. To give them hope and just be a role model.

JENNIFER CAPRIATI
Fort Lauderdale Sun-Sentinel (December 2, 2001)

Who knows if I would have gotten to number one if everything had gone like it was supposed to. Maybe that's why things happened the way they did—to make me appreciate and understand my life.

JENNIFER CAPRIATI
Fort Lauderdale Sun-Sentinel (December 2, 2001)

If I see the ball on the line, I would give the ball to the opponent, that's for sure, no matter if it's the final or first round.

ALEX CORRETJA, ATP PLAYER (2001)

When I began my career, my sister was very sick. I played for her to raise some money. . . . Then the war came and I played for the people who were fighting for my country. After that I had to find somebody to play for, but I couldn't. So I said, "Man, after twelve years on the Tour, I think you deserve to play for yourself a little bit."

GORAN IVANISEVIC (2001)
BBC Sport

I play to raise money to help support my family in Russia.

MARAT SAFIN, ATP PLAYER

Andy Roddick, on occasion, hammers when a feather-touch is required. His juices get the best of him.

SELENA ROBERTS
The New York Times (September 3, 2001)

———

We grew up practicing together. When she was doing well I wanted to do the same. I wanted to be on top, be a grand slam champion. I wanted to be the best. That's what I am working for.

SERENA WILLIAMS, REFERRING TO HER SISTER (2001)

When Connors played you knew he was going to rip open his chest and leave his guts on the court.

SAL PAOLANTONIO
ESPN radio (September 10, 2001)

It's much more enjoyable watching him than playing against him . . . Sometimes you feel like you're watching when you're out there playing against him because he really hits some shots that you just can't believe a person can even attempt, let alone make.

ANDRE AGASSI, ON ANDRE ILIE, 2002 AUSTRALIAN OPEN

Edberg has never ducked a tournament. From Australia, to France, to England, to the US, in heat, in rain, in chill, on grass, on clay, on hard courts. Edberg always has shown up, a Cal Ripken of tennis.

GEORGE VECSEY, ON STEFAN EDBERG'S FIFTY-FOUR CONSECUTIVE
GRAND SLAM APPEARANCES
The New York Times (September 4, 1996)

No teenager has made a bigger impact on his first Centre Court appearance since Boris Becker in 1985 . . . and Roddick's charming approach continued long after he won even more hearts by patiently signing autographs as he left the scene of his victory.

JOHN PARSONS, ON ANDY RODDICK (2001)
London Daily Telegraph

It's not his talent as much as his versatility.

PAT MCENROE, US DAVIS CUP COACH, ON ANDY RODDICK, MONTREAL 2001

He knows the crowd loves him, and he responds in a nice way. Women are just crazy about Pat. I mean, my wife is ready to leave me for him.

BUD COLLINS, ON PAT RAFTER
People (August 31, 1998)

When Dennis Ralston was performing at the top of his game he made the game look like it was invented for him. A superb server and volleyer, his ground strokes flowed, his footwork was exemplary, his touch exquisite.

STEVE FINK
Tennis Week (October 25, 2001)

Arthur Ashe is the soul of tennis, whose contributions know no bounds. He is my all-time number one player in any sport.

NEIL AMDUR
World Tennis (December 1989)

———

Exemplifying the game of tennis, she has figured out everything about the game, she understands the symmetry of the court and the timing.

PHILIPPE BOUIN, TENNIS WRITER, ON MARTINA HINGIS
L'Equipe

Hingis's slow serve is room service.

DICK ENBERG, CBS SPORTS COMMENTATOR, 2001 U.S. OPEN

Hingis believes she can beat all the other women, the ones who are bigger, stronger and faster, the ones who pulverize her second serve, the ones who close down her clever angles, the ones who pummel her with their relentless ground strokes.

DIANE PUCIN
Los Angeles Times (September 7, 2001)

We were playing doubles and she hit this unbelievably difficult backhand volley. I asked her where she got it. She said Gigi Fernandaz hit it once, so she went home and asked her mother to teach her that shot. If I asked my coach to teach me that shot, it would take me ten years.

LINDSAY DAVENPORT, ON MARTINA HINGIS
The New York Times (August 24, 1997)

I think I am playing the best ever, so it's kind of funny. I was such an early starter, early prodigy, but I feel like a late bloomer.

JENNIFER CAPRIATI, ON HER 2001 SUCCESS
The New York Times (August 19, 2001)

She tends to lose her rhythm, either going for too much at 90 percent power and being too wild or backing down too much at 50 percent power. She needs to hit more shots at 75 percent power.

TRACY AUSTIN, FORMER WTA PLAYER, ON SERENA WILLIAMS, U.S. OPEN 2001
USA Network

Margaret Court had a tremendous ability to push herself, she wanted to achieve, she was always asking what can I do to improve.

KEITH ROGERS, COACH OF MARGARET COURT
Court on Court by Margaret Smith Court

... the most ill-tempered, petulant loudmouth that the game of tennis has ever known.

The Sun (London tabloid), on John McEnroe (1980)

McEnroe questioned seventeen calls; know how many were close enough for a second glance? Two. The others he was just bitching. Maybe he is doing it to fire himself up, maybe it's to upset the other guy, but don't give me that stuff that he is doing it because he is a perfectionist.

ROD FRAWLEY, ON HIS WIMBELDON SEMIFINALS MATCH AGAINST
MCENROE
Short Circuit by Michael Mewshaw

His knowledge on how to use the whole service box with his variety of serve spins and speeds is part of his genius.

DICK ENBERG, ON PETE SAMPRAS (2001)
CBS Sports

Tim Gullikson was such a verbal guy he put Sampras in touch with what tennis was all about, he gave Pete a tremendous boost in terms of technique and strategy, but he also made tennis real in Pete's life.

PETER BODO, TENNIS WRITER
Sampras: A Legend in the Works by H. A. Branham

Sampras is starting to realize what it means to grow old in the game. It means creaky joints and subtle breakdowns, but it also means the full measure of appreciation. . . Long known for his dull, slouchy demeanor on court, Sampras seems to be winning people over—finally.

BRUCE JENKINS
San Francisco Chronicle (September 4, 2001)

In men's tennis it's Sampras and everyone else. Sure, the other guys: Agassi, Rafter, Todd Martin, Safin can win. But when they do, it's considered an upset . . . because he's so good at what he does and the way he does it.

WARNER WOLFE, SPORTSCASTER
Let's Go to the Videotape!

———

There is nothing boring about such depthless ambition or utter all-time greatness.

SALLY JENKINS, ON SAMPRAS
Inside Tennis Yearbook (2002)

It was a pure go-for-the-jugular shot of adrenaline. Unleashing an almost primal ferocity, he launched into every game, every point with popping intensity.

WILLIAM SIMONS, ON JIMMY CONNORS
Inside Tennis (September 10, 2001)

He was once said to be the best man playing women's tennis. In fact, Jimmy Connors plays tennis the way every champion has, and he found that style natural to him early in life and stuck to it.

CATHERINE BELL AND ROY PETERS
Passing Shots

Jimmy Connors loved to compete, he couldn't wait to get out there.

CLIFF DRYSDALE
ESPN (2001)

In terms of romance with the U.S. Open crowd, Agassi falls in with the Connors, McEnroe category. Not because he's periodically a jerk, but because of his flamboyance, the way he shares his emotions with the fans.

H.A. BRANHAM
Sampras: A Legend in the Works

I'm very extreme, when I am focused I am very focused, when I am distracted, I am very distracted.

ANDRE AGASSI
Inside Tennis (September 9, 2001)

Monica Seles, hands down, is the nicest player on tour. Most players, when you get them what they need, go about their business and are more or less friendly. Monica is always: May I please have this, thank you very much, you girls are doing a great job.

KRISTIN AGDEN, BALL PERSON FOR EIGHT YEARS
Tennis Week (October 23, 2001)

He has the physical strength to hit his way through nervousness. That's why I believe he is a great player.

FREW MCMILLAN, FORMER MEN'S TOUR PLAYER, ON ROD LAVER
"Centre Court" by John McPhee, *Playboy* (June 1971)

All the women who hit a one-handed backhand are not that strong. But Justine Henin plays so great from her one-handed backhand. It's the best one-handed backhand I have ever seen.

LINA KRASNOROUTSKAYA, WTA PLAYER (2001)

Agassi is Reggie Jackson, Sampras is Harmon Killebrew.

SCOTT OSTLER, AFTER THE SYBASE TOURNAMENT IN SAN JOSE,
CALIFORNIA, WHERE SAMPRAS BEAT AGASSI
San Francisco Chronicle (February 1996)

Usually Gustavo Kuerten can find the rip cord when a match starts to fall apart; spiraling out of control and hope is all but gone. He is one of the best at soft landings and narrow escapes.

SELENA ROBERTS
The New York Times (September 7, 2001)

A belated national champion. After years of playing on the Black American Tennis Association Circuit, Gibson played a powerful athletic serve and volley style. In the process she overcame the racial and social obstacles and won the most prestigious titles in the game.

NEIL AMDUR, ON ALTHEA GIBSON

———

When Billie Jean King played she acted like she should win every point; she was a perfectionist.

CLIFF DRYSDALE
ESPN, October 12, 1989

Billie Jean is the greatest competitor that I have ever known. Although I considered her forehand her weak shot, I played her down the middle so as not to give her the wide ball she loves.

MARGARET SMITH COURT
Court on Court, A Life in Tennis

If all of the tennis players who ever lived were wiped from human memory and only Billie Jean King remained, you could reconstruct from the perfection of the technique the complete competitor.

CATHERINE BELL AND ROY PETERS
Passing Shots

Every woman on the tour should walk up to Billie Jean King and say thank you. For she single-handedly made women's professional tennis what it is.

CHRIS EVERT
Bravo Biography: Billie Jean King (March 4, 2002)

Ion Tiriac did not resemble a tennis player. He appears to be a Panatela ad, a triple agent from Alexandria, a used car salesman from Central Marrakish.

JOHN MCPHEE
"Centre Court," *Playboy* (June 1971)

Tom Okker's quickness and agility earned him the nickname of The Flying Dutchman. His nervous manner and inability to sit still won him the title of Tom the Twitch.

ROBERT SLATER
Great Jews in Sports

The biggest weapon in men's tennis was Mats Wilander's brain.

JAY BERGER, FORMER ATP PLAYER

My mom wasn't pretentious. She was a real person. She usually wore sweatpants and never had any scrap-book of her meteoric career around the house . . . We didn't talk about tennis . . . She didn't want us to feel the pressure of following in the footsteps of a famous parent.

CINDY BRINKER-SIMMONS, AUTHOR
Little Mo's Legacy: A Mother's Lessons

Lacoste reduced defense to a mathematical science, he has developed his defense to the state when it becomes an offense in the pressure it brings to bear as the ball is sent back deeper and deeper and into more and more remote territory.

ALLISON DANZIG, FORMER *THE NEW YORK TIMES* TENNIS WRITER
The Right Set, edited by Caryl Phillips

There is no other player I more enjoyed watching. There was no player more conscious of the crowd. She was the most outrageous ham on the circuit.

GRACE LICHTENSTEIN, ON ROSIE CASALS
A Long Way, Baby

What made her most attractive on the court was her demeanor. She never scolded, never argued, hardly ever showed a tinge of regret over a miss-hit. She splashed around the court with a giddy delight.

GRACE LICHTENSTEIN, ON EVONNE GOOLAGONG
A Long Way, Baby

She held her racquet in a peculiar way, showing that conventional wisdom tennis instruction wastes time trying to make people look less goofy.

ROBERT FIRLUS, ON FRANCOISE DURR
Tennis Week (June 26, 2001)

Chris Evert won many tournaments because her backhand was absolutely reliable. Every great champion has a certain way of hitting the ball which is signature. This is how Chris signed herself into history.

CATHERINE BELL AND ROY PETERS
Passing Shots

By remaining true to herself, Jimmy Evert's little girl gave a new meaning to the title World Champion.

NEIL AMDUR, ON CHRIS EVERT
World Tennis (December 1989)

No one in the history of tennis has played the game so skillfully and successfully for so long without interruption as Evert.

STEVE FINK
World Tennis (December 1989)

———

Lleyton Hewitt has been on a remarkable pace. . . You have to go back to Borg or Becker to find someone who has achieved this much so quickly.

TOM ROSS, LLEYTON HEWITT'S AGENT
San Francisco Chronicle (February 24, 2002)

Tennis needs Lleyton Hewitt's finesse and work ethic. It needs a shot maker to act as a counterpoint to the six-foot-four crushers who make up the bulk of the top players.

CHARLES BRINKER
Fort Lauderdale Sun-Sentinel (November 25, 2001)

She does nothing to beat herself. She beats the players she should beat and half of the players she shouldn't.

DR. DARRELL HOFFMAN, REFERRING TO HIS DAUGHTER SARAH, TOP
NOR-CAL PLAYER AND NATIONAL JUNIOR

Rosewall was among the top five players ever and pound for pound the best player ever.

PETER ROWLEY
Ken Rosewall: Twenty Years at the Top

———•◦•◦•———

Rosewall is never off. He has you crazy when you are serving because his return is so good. You know if you miss the first serve you can forget the point so you press so hard not to miss it, that you miss it.

FRED STOLLE, FORMER MEN'S TOUR PLAYER
Ken Rosewall: Twenty Years at the Top by Peter Rowley

I wanted to behave like him on court. I had seen him several times on television and had been terribly impressed by this player who never said a word and whose concentration was always so perfect. Yes, he was the example I chose to follow.

BJORN BORG, ON ROD LAVER
www.bjornborg.20m.com

Three things I remember about Ivan Lendl: the Foreign Legion hat, the sawdust in his pocket, and he would not play if anyone in the stadium was moving.

TED ROBINSON, COMMENTATOR
USA Network (2001)

When I was a kid I saw Rafter play Albert Costa. Rafter was fighting like a dog and Costa was playing unbelievable. I hope that's the impression I am giving out there—fighting like a dog win or lose. I want to have Rafter's intensity and will on the court.

TAYLOR DENT, ATP PLAYER, AT WIMBLEDON 2001

When Boris Becker played, you could touch his emotions.

CLIFF DRYSDALE
ESPN, Australian Open 2002

Only five feet eleven inches, which is hardly the standard size for a big server, he makes up for it with superior technique: bending his knees deeply, driving up into the ball and keeping his toss just the right distance in front of him.

CHRISTOPHER CLAREY, ON THOMAS JOHANSSON
The New York Times (January 28, 2002)

She never missed. She had accurate passing shots. She could run forever and moved beautifully. She was so tough on big points. People used to say she had ice in her veins.

LOUISE BROUGH, FORMER WOMEN'S TOUR PLAYER, ON PAULINE BETZ
Tennis Week (March 7, 2002)

Her shots felt like they'd been dipped in concrete, probably because she used a fifteen-ounce racquet, almost twice as heavy as many of today's racquets.

JOSEPH STAHL, ON HELEN WILLS MOODY
Tennis Week (March 7, 2002)

The crowd loves the blood and guts style of tennis. They cheer for him as he fights for every point.

JIM SARNI, ON WHY THE U.S. OPEN CROWD LOVED CONNORS
Fort Lauderdale Sun-Sentinel (September 6, 1988)

His athleticism is a big key to his success and so is his in-your-face tactics. It doesn't matter how big you hit or who you are. Every time you look up, Rafter is at the net challenging you to make a passing shot.

CHARLES BRINKER
Fort Lauderdale Sun-Sentinel (September 14, 1998)

By almost any yardstick, bigger is better in the world of tennis, but smaller players, like Hewitt, Grosjean and Henin proved that with great legs and hard work it is possible to slam the giants.

CHARLES BRINKER
Fort Lauderdale Sun-Sentinel (March 20, 2002)

Nastase was insulted by the calls or non-calls of the lineman. He replied with a string of obscene words and gestures but no one complained. From beginning to end he kept the crowd applauding, laughing, hollering and occasionally booing.

STEPHANIE SLATER, ON A NASTASE TEAM TENNIS MATCH
Nasty: Ilie Nastase vs Tennis by Richard Evans

Nastase projects an image on court of Dracula. People love to come and shudder when he approaches the baseline—brandishing a racquet at the umpire or going after a heckler.

JIM MURRAY
Nasty: Ilie Nastase vs Tennis by Richard Evans

As his gestures on the court indicate, he has no idea where to find the line that divides funny, risqué humor from obscenity.

RICHARD EVANS, ON JIMMY CONNORS
Nasty: Ilie Nastase vs Tennis by Richard Evans

Vitas Gerualaitis was to tennis what Joe Namath was to football. Both operated in the spotlight. Gerulaitis's generous demeanor, lively post-match banter and dynamic playing style seemed to mirror the mercurial attitude of the city he represented.

NEIL AMDUR
The New York Times (September 22, 1994)

He combined power, touch and tennis sense as few players before him had done. Saturnine and disputatious, an unrepentant loner, this tall graceful man who moved like a panther seemed to forever have a chip on his shoulder.

HERBERT WARREN WIND, ON PANCHO GONZALEZ
Game, Set, and Match by Herbert Warren Wind

Connors reminds us all of how much we have given up growing old. If only we could make grown-ups applaud our naughty words, dance through the hors d'oeuvres, posture and preen and be a terrible two. The only time a human being will be loved for conquering the world crying.

ROBERT LIPSYTE
The New York Times (September 8, 1991)

The players know in the locker room that if you can stay with Marat Safin, he may crumble under the pressure.

CLIFF DRYSDALE
ESPN (March 28, 2002)

What used to astound me about Bjorn Borg was his ability to turn defense into offense when he was pressured.

CLIFF DRYSDALE
ESPN (March 24, 2002)

Tilden always seems to have a thousand means of putting the ball away. Sometimes he gives the ball tremendous velocity. Sometimes he caresses it, directing it to a spot on the court nobody but he himself would have thought to direct it.

RENEE LACOSTE, SEVEN-TIME GRAND SLAM CHAMPION
Game, Set, and Match by Herbert Warren Wind

Over the last few years Agassi's serve is vastly improved. You don't see many players late in their career improve a skill so much.

CLIFF BUCKHOLTZ, DIRECTOR, NASDAQ 100 TOURNAMENT
ESPN (March 25, 2002)

She is probably one of the last serve-and-volleyers on the women's side. It was unreal how she and Martina Navratilova played doubles dominating and intimidating in one of the best combos ever.

HANK HARRIS, PAM SHRIVER'S COACH, ON PAM SHRIVER
The New York Times (August 28, 1996)

Maureen's court demeanor was amazing. Years later people talked about how Chris Evert was so mentally strong on the court. Well, Maureen was ten times better.

DORIS HART, FORMER WOMEN'S TOUR PLAYER, ON MAUREEN CONNOLLY
Tennis Week (April 2, 2002)

It was always an art and act I came to perfect. It was part of my armory. I felt if my opponent didn't know what I was thinking then I was invincible.

BJORN BORG, ON HIS EXTREME STOICISM
Inside Tennis (April 2002)

Certain players would rather die than default a match. That's the kind of player Jimmy was. You had to drag him off the court.

CHRIS EVERT, ON JIMMY CONNORS
The New York Times (July 12, 1998)

The name of the game John McEnroe always played best was "surprise." Where was the next volley going to go? When was the inevitable tantrum coming? What Robin Williams is to comedy, McEnroe was to tennis. He made it up as he went along.

HARVEY ARATON
The New York Times (July 11, 1999)

Her game may be mature beyond years but her behaviour was a very public temper tantrum and her offenses were definitely booable offenses. She was the author of the atmosphere. She turned a grand slam final into a Jerry Springer festival.

MARY CARILLO, FORMER WTA PLAYER, ON HINGIS'S MELTDOWN AT 1999 FRENCH OPEN FINAL
The New York Times (June 20, 1999)

––•••––

If you needed a quote you went to Ted Tinling. The man knew more about tennis than anyone and he could express it better than anyone.

JIM SARNI
Fort Lauderdale Sun-Sentinel (May 27, 1990)

As a boy he was a natural athlete, and his passion was baseball. Perhaps because he was a right-handed thrower and a left-handed batter, he developed a backhand that has never been equaled.

ROBERT MINTON, ON DON BUDGE
Forest Hills: An Illustrated History

His serve was battering, his backhand perhaps the finest the game has known, his net play emphatic—quick and rhythmic. He was an all-around player whose concentration could not be shaken.

BUD COLLINS, ON DON BUDGE
Bud Collins' Modern Encyclopedia of Tennis

Vines' power was frightening . . . one of his smashes hit a ball boy in the chest and knocked him head over heels. The lanky Californian's services were timed at 128 miles per hour.

UNITED STATES LAWN TENNIS ASSOCIATION OFFICIAL ENCYCLOPEDIA
OF TENNIS
ON ELLSWORTH VINES, THREE-TIME GRAND SLAM CHAMPION

Jimmy Connors doesn't like to lose, not even in practice.

JIMMY ARIAS, FORMER ATP PLAYER
Days of Grace: A Memoir by Arthur Ashe

Lew Hoad was the best male player I ever saw. He could be absolutely phenomenal and devastating in his day. He had a carefree attitude so he got beaten by some ordinary players.

ALAN TRENGOVE
Tennis Week (June 26, 2001)

He handles my power better than anyone in the world. I laced some balls [today], just hit them really hard, and he got them back.

ANDY RODDICK, ATP PLAYER, ON LLEYTON HEWITT, U.S. OPEN 2001
St. Petersburg Times (September 8, 2001)

Hewitt runs down everything, so you have to hit three or four really good shots until the point is over.

THOMAS JOHANSSON, ATP PLAYER (2001)
www.daviscup.org

He is the perfect combination of raw power and great touch.

TIM GULLIKSON, ON PETE SAMPRAS
Pete Sampras by Calvin Craig Miller

Guga hasn't lost any of the surfer dudosity he showed up with when he first emerged. Guga is a human slinky who has a backhand swing that starts in Kentucky and ends in Ohio.

MARY CARILLO, FORMER WTA PLAYER, ON GUSTAVO KUERTEN
(2001)

People say Lleyton Hewitt and Andy should have a great rivalry but how can you have a great rivalry if one guy wins all the time?

ANDY RODDICK, ATP PLAYER
Tennis (December 2001)

Brad's got a good heart but I couldn't take all the talking, discussing every angle, every shot when we practice. I would say to Brad, "Could you shut up for thirty minutes?"

PETE SAMPRAS, ON BRAD GILBERT
Agassi & Ecstasy by Paul Bauman

Zina Garrison ended my career by beating me in the 1989 Open quarterfinals. I can't think of anyone else I would have wanted standing across the net at that moment. Zina doesn't have a mean bone in her body.

CHRIS EVERT
Sports Illustrated (1989)

He's an old has-been, who can't see, he can't hear, he walks like a duck, and he is an idiot besides.

ROSIE CASALS, FORMER WTA PLAYER, ON BOBBY RIGGS
A Long Way, Baby by Grace Lichtenstein

One of my biggest highlights of my career is having my brother on the court with me in mixed doubles.

JENNIFER CAPRIATI, AT U.S. OPEN 2001

Tiriac used to say he was the best tennis player who could not play tennis. Grotesque, gritty, grubbing and grasping he had the right talent. He wanted so badly to beat most opponents including his betters.

BUD COLLINS
Sampras: A Legend in the Works by H. A. Branham

We loved Bill. Temperamental, strange, generous—he was the king and always will be to those who loved the game.

ALICE MARBLE, FIVE-TIME GRAND SLAM CHAMPION, ON BILL TILDEN
World Tennis by Richard Evans and John Haylett

When Max Mirnyi hits his first serve in at 125 miles per hour, I don't care how good your return is, it is not coming back.

YEVGENY KAFELNIKOV, ATP PLAYER (2001)

Since Althea was black, she was having a difficult time getting a doubles partner in America. And since I was Jewish, I was having a similar problem in England. So we just hooked up.

ANGELA BURTON, BRITISH TENNIS PRO, ON ALTHEA GIBSON
Great Jews in Sports by Robert Slater

One thing that amazes me about Pete is how he believes in himself. He believes he is better and supposed to win. Even those times he is in a slump he doesn't waver.

PAUL ANNACONE, AT U.S. OPEN 2001

Crowds have cheered champions who had fits of bad temper and ill manners. Like Connors and McEnroe. When fans were treated to great performances by Sampras, who didn't engage in this kind of behavior, people called him a bore.

JOHN FEINSTEIN
Pete Sampras by Calvin Craig Miller

He has the power, he has the speed he has the touch—
he is the best player ever.

CALVIN CRAIG MILLER, ON SAMPRAS
Pete Sampras

It is so hard to remain positive against Sampras
because you have so few chances.

JOHN MCENROE (2001)
CBS Sports

It's incredible how focused Andre is and the pace at which he plays. Even in practice his hands are fast, his feet are fast. The points go by so fast.

ANDY RODDICK, ATP PLAYER, ON AGASSI
Tennis (December 2001)

Brad's made a career out of winning matches he was supposed to lose. Up to this point in my career I have done the opposite.

ANDRE AGASSI
Agassi and Ecstasy by Paul Bauman

He doesn't get fast points like Sampras. He really has to work from the baseline. To do that for over ten years that's an unbelievable thing.

ROGER FEDERER, ATP PLAYER, ON AGASSI, AT U.S. OPEN 2001

———

Andre in '93 would have gotten smoked by the Andre of today at thirty-one.

BRAD GILBERT, AGASSI'S COACH AT U.S. OPEN 2001

Steffi Graf . . . best footwork in tennis . . . man or woman.

BRAD GILBERT (2001)
ESPN

———————

It's the discipline of her life, it's the loyalty of her heart, it's the generosity of her spirit. Every day you're around her, the more amazed you are by her.

ANDRE AGASSI, ON STEFFI GRAF
Inside Tennis (September 2001)

He is the best returner in the game, even better than Andre, because he is quicker and simply doesn't miss. He also has the best wheels in the game. What I'd give to have those legs.

PETE SAMPRAS, ON LLEYTON HEWITT, AT U.S. OPEN 2001

I didn't serve to Rosewall's backhand. I would usually go to his forehand and I tried to return to his forehand volley. His whole backhand side was deadly.

TONY ROCHE, FORMER MEN'S TOUR PLAYER
Ken Rosewall: Twenty Years at the Top by Peter Rowley

He is one of the few players who can hit anyone off the court.

TODD MARTIN, ATP PLAYER ON MARAT SAFIN (2001)

———————

I probably respect Monica Seles more than any other player out there. Not only as a player but as a good friend and an amazing person.

LINDSAY DAVENPORT, AFTER DEFEATING MONICA SELES IN LOS ANGELES (2001)
Estyle.com

I draw confidence from looking at a guy like Andre Agassi. He can beat any player on any given day on any surface.

LLEYTON HEWITT, ATP PLAYER
The New York Times (February 24, 2002)

———

Her physicality could overwhelm you, her attitude on the court intimidated players, she was expressive, always moving, yelling, screaming, demanding attention.

CHRIS EVERT, ON BILLIE JEAN KING
Chrissie: My Own Story by Chris Evert with Neil Amdur

When Ivan Lendl was trying to join the American Davis Cup Team, John McEnroe said he couldn't swallow it if Lendl were to become a Davis Cup teammate. Lendl said he thought McEnroe's mouth was big enough to swallow anything.

JIM SARNI
Fort Lauderdale Sun-Sentinel (September 9, 1987)

When Ken Rosewall misses a backhand down the line by an inch and drops his racquet in disgust, he is annoyed because hitting that backhand with absolute perfection is his craft, and when he misses, it just burns him inside. It's called the pride of performance.

RICHARD EVANS
Nasty: Ilie Nastase vs Tennis by Richard Evans

For Ilie Nastase bad line calls were a curse, delivered from some supreme tennis being out to destroy him. Thus his arms frequently gestured to the heavens.

CHRIS EVERT
Chrissie: My Own Story by Chris Evert with Neil Amdur

Evonne was a moody player. If the mood struck her, she could play exquisitely a feathery brand of tennis that no one could duplicate. There were days she couldn't move her feet.

CHRIS EVERT, ON EVONNE GOOLAGONG
Chrissie: My Own Story by Chris Evert and Neil Amdur

When I walk out to play Boris Becker, he brings an aura with him. When we play it is always a packed house, which adds a bit more to that match. We have grown to respect each other on and off the court.

PETE SAMPRAS
International Tennis (March 1, 1998)

He is the one person I learned the most from. In his style of how to play, to the way he handles himself on the court, he has definitely been an inspiration.

TIM HENMAN, ATP PLAYER, ON STEFAN EDBERG
The New York Times (September 4, 1996)

Even when I am practicing good, I don't believe in myself. I should believe in myself that I can play better, then it will come out when I play.

AI SUGIYAMA, WTA PLAYER (2001)

Stefan Edberg has defined himself as a serve and volley player, and you cannot shake him off that concept.

TIM GULLIKSON, LATE COACH OF PETE SAMPRAS, AT THE 1991
NEWSWEEK TOURNAMENT

The Mind Game

Tennis is simple. If you don't have self esteem, you lose. Tennis is about head, then legs, then shots.

CHUCK KRIESE, TENNIS COACH
Tough Draw by Eliot Berry

I need to be able to laugh at everything I do—whether it's training or whatever, smiling helps me relax.

VIRGINIA RAZZANO, WTA PLAYER

Being Little Mo's daughter and playing on her turf taught me how to thrive on pressure. . . It made me work harder. It also became a way to shield myself from the pain of Mom's loss.

CINDY BRINKER
Little Mo's Legacy: A Mother's Lessons

What noise?

TOM GULLIKSON, WHEN ASKED HOW HE COULD FOCUS WELL ENOUGH
TO WIN A FOUR-SET U.S. OPEN MATCH AGAINST CHIP HOOPER WITH
THE NOISE OF PLANES FLYING OVERHEAD EVERY THIRTY SECONDS
The Corporate Athlete by Dr. Jack Groppel

I am superstitious about not being superstitious.

TAYLOR DENT, ATP PLAYER (2001)

If I am winning, I take the same shower and sit on the same side of the court every match.

KATHERINE ADAMS
WTA official Web site (www.wtatour.com)

If I win a match, I eat the same food every day. At Wimbledon I had chicken and fruit for two weeks.

JUSTINE HENIN, WTA PLAYER (2001)

Tony Roche is a very superstitious character who claims he wore the same pair of tennis shorts for two years while he was winning. A hotel lost the shorts and Roche lost his very next match.

MARTY BELL
Carnival at Forest Hills

I am going to try and just have some fun. I do my best when I just have fun.

SERENA WILLIAMS (2001)

———•••———

If you really want to achieve something in your life, whatever you do to achieve the goal is not a sacrifice. It is something you have to do.

CHRIS EVERT
Chrissie by Chris Evert and Neil Amdur

In practice Chris kills me. When I asked him why he can't play like that in a match, he said, "I can't get myself to relax like this in a match."

JIM COURIER, ON PRACTICING WITH CHRIS WOODRUFF
HBO (2001)

One of the signs of nervousness is the abandoning of your game plan.

MAL WASHINGTON
ESPN (2002)

The great players can identify the important points in a match and then step up the play one more notch.

LEIF SHIRAS
Outdoor Living Network (March 2, 2002)

Always something interesting going on with me when I play, some aces, a little talking, a little fighting, a little racquet throwing. It's like an action film. This is how I win.

GORAN IVANISEVIC, ATP PLAYER
The New York Times (September 2, 1996)

The fans won me more matches than I can tell you. I think they liked my working-man style. People who did not know tennis related to it, whether they were for me or against me.

JIMMY CONNORS
The New York Times (July 12, 1998)

I have a lot of recurring dreams about that match. I will think about it the rest of my life.

JOHN MCENROE, ON LOSING TO IVAN LENDL IN THE 1984 FRENCH OPEN FINALS WHEN HE WAS UP TWO SETS
Fort Lauderdale Sun-Sentinel (May 30, 1988)

I'm the kind of player who is not very much motivated by money or wins or by anything. Until I feel good or until I feel that I want to play, nobody can push me. I'm the only one who's in charge of that.

ANDREI MEDVEDEV, ATP PLAYER (2001)
www.asapsports.com

Sometimes when I play too good I get bored, so I invent new shots.

GORAN IVANISEVIC, ATP PLAYER (2001)

You've got to block everything out, especially if you think you are winning—when I win a set I start to think about the next match instead of one point at a time—if you let your mind go for a second that's when you lose it in this game.

MARTIN LEE, ATP PLAYER, AT WIMBLEDON (2001)

If you are playing here and you are negative, you need to go see a shrink.

CEDRIC PIOLINE, ATP PLAYER, AT ROLAND GARROS (2001)

Tennis parents are most important where the child loses—you try to have empathy with them, you understand what they are going through. You love them no matter what happens—you make sure that the experience is making them stronger not weaker.

JIM LOEHR, SPORTS PSYCHOLOGIST
Ladies of the Court by Michael Mewshaw

To tennis parents: If you are the source of pressure you are missing the point—a parent's role is to provide support, love and care.

JIM LOEHR, SPORTS PSYCHOLOGIST
Ladies of the Court by Michael Mewshaw

You always think you can win a match—if not, don't step onto the court.

GASTON GAUDIO, ATP PLAYER (2001)

I have to play a tournament as good as I play in practice. It sounds simple, but it's not.

PATTY SCHNYDER, WTA PLAYER (2001)

The game is very much between the ears—I am content to admit I can get tight sometimes, but it is how you deal with it that matters.

TIM HENMAN, ATP PLAYER (2001)

A magnificent shot which beats him completely doesn't cause a player mental anguish. He will admire it and not worry about it. But each time he sees an important shot miss, he becomes more nervous and less likely to win.

BILL TILDEN
Big Bill Tilden by Frank Deford

When you find yourself on the court and you are not doing exactly what you want to do—you see opportunities that you do not take. The opponent has nothing to do with that. It's between you and yourself.

CEDRIC PIOLINE, ATP PLAYER (2001)

The opponent is not on the other side of the net—it is between your ears.

ANTONY PAZ, TENNIS COACH

You can't play good tennis if what you are thinking about is how other people are perceiving you.

U.S. SENATOR BOB GRAHAM
www.nytimes.com (June 21, 2002)

———•••••———

The thrill in tennis is being able to sit down, plot out a strategy and be able to do it on a court—whether it is Court 800 with no one watching or Court 1 in front of thousands. It's the idea of being able to train your attention, your concentration, and focus.

CECE MARTINEZ, FORMER WTA TOUR PLAYER
A Long Way, Baby by Grace Lichtenstein

Think long term. Risk losing while you let yourself become comfortable with your new shots and each match will be less threatening than the last.

JEFF GREENWALD, CLINICAL PSYCHOLOGIST
Tennis (December 2001)

When you invest so much time and energy in tennis, it is hard to detach your feelings of self-worth from the results. This makes winning more important and losing that much harder.

JULIE ANTHONY, FORMER WTA PLAYER, NOW A PSYCHOLOGIST
Tennis (December 2001)

A man who waits to believe in action before acting is anything you like, but he's not a man of action. It is as if a tennis player, before returning a ball, stopped to think about his views of the physical and mental advantages of tennis. You must act as you breathe.

GEORGES CLEMENCEAU, IN A CONVERSATION WITH JEAN MARET (1927)
Respectfully quoted from the Library of Congress

If you get to know a player too well (as in friendship), the fear is that you end up playing against her personality more than her game.

VANESSA WEHLS, WTA PLAYER
Venus Envy by L. Jon Wertheim

———

Venus told me, "Great players don't get nervous, they pull it out," and that's the way I am trying to be. I don't have time to be nervous anymore.

SERENA WILLIAMS (2001)

I was smashing twenty racquets a year. I was just angry and got too frustrated when things were not going my way.

MARTIN LEE, ATP PLAYER, ON WHY HE SEES A SPORTS PSYCHIATRIST

Even when I was winning there would be ten points that I was angry the way I won the point. Now I am happy as long as I win the point.

MARTIN LEE, ATP PLAYER, ON HIS TEMPER

I realized that racquet throwing didn't help my game because I was always getting negative. I used to negative talk, now I don't talk.

ROGER FEDERER, ATP PLAYER (2001)

I used to throw my racquet like you probably can't imagine. It was like helicopters flying all over. I was getting kicked out of practice at age sixteen nonstop. Now I have learned to relax on the court.

ROGER FEDERER, ATP PLAYER (2001)

I do it for me, for myself. If the public enjoys it, so much the better.

ILIE NASTASE, ON ACTING UP ON THE COURT
Short Circuit by Michael Mewshaw

———

When I run out of excuses.

BETSY HOLAK, USTA PLAYER, WHEN ASKED WHEN SHE WAS GOING TO START TO PLAY UP TO HER ABILITY

All whining, negative thinking and excuses must be eliminated from your game. Winning can't be controlled, but the "I can win" attitude can and needs to be.

DR. JOHN F. MOLLY, SPORTS PSYCHOLOGIST
Tennis (December 2001)

Key psychological factors in tennis and life development include the development of a work ethic and discipline, accommodation of stress, improved problem solving, the ability to plan and implement strategies, tactics and the development of positive rituals in your life.

DR. JACK GROPPEL, SPORTS MEDICINE DOCTOR
USPTA magazine (December 2001)

Tennis players scored higher in vigor, optimism and self esteem while scoring lower in depression, anger, confusion, anxiety and tension than other athletes.

DR. JOHN FINN, SPORTS PSYCHOLOGIST
USPTA magazine (November 2001)

Chris Woodruff, ATP player, Wimbledon (2001)

I am trying to play the match point by point—instead of worrying what the score is or the surroundings. It is the only thing I can control.

CHRIS WOODRUFF, ATP PLAYER, WIMBLEDON (2001)

Between points, 90 percent of the time I am looking at my coach. I am not very self-confident, so I need this type of feedback. I can tell what he is thinking by just looking at him.

ANTHONY DUPUIS, ATP PLAYER (2001)

———

I thought if I lose, it doesn't matter. At least I enjoyed myself. This is not normal thinking. I think it is more normal to break a racquet or cry.

ARNAUD CLEMENT, ATP PLAYER, ROLAND GARROS (2001)

I believe I can be a better tennis player than I am now. I also believe that I can be better than I ever was before. But until I find that happy place inside me, I don't think I can do it.

ANDREI MEDVEDEV, ATP PLAYER (2001)

I am not playing Martina, I am playing the ball.

CHRIS EVERT, WHEN ASKED IF SHE WAS TIRED OF PLAYING
NAVRATILOVA AFTER LOSING THIRTEEN STRAIGHT TIMES TO HER

Because I am small I will never a have a big serve or hit very hard. My weapon is to play tactically well and have good touch.

OLIVER ROCHUS, ATP PLAYER (2001)

You try and beat the hell out of the opponent—then shake hands when it is over.

IVAN LENDL (2001)

Being competitive and having a killer instinct are two different things; there is a vast difference between wanting to beat an opponent and wanting to kill her. With the killer instinct you never give the opponent the opportunity or reason to believe they could win the match.

MARTINA NAVRATILOVA
The Right Set edited by Caryl Phillips

I was taught that once you got up in a match you tried to grab the opponent by the throat and finish him off.

IVAN LENDL (2001)

I have to be more patient, which is more draining physically than mentally.

FABRICE SANTORO, ATP PLAYER (2001)

———•••———

Players with high risk-tolerance do not become as nervous as most people in risky situations—in fact, the risky important situations excite and stimulate them. It gets their adrenaline going; they get pumped up.

ALLEN FOX, PSYCHOLOGIST
Tennis Week (October 23, 2001)

When I was down 4–2 in the fourth I thought it was over—the crowd was heavily against me but one guy in the crowd kept yelling for me. He wanted me to win so badly I could see him suffering every time I lost a point. It helped me because it gave me a reason to fight.

ILIE NASTASE, ON HIS U.S. OPEN WIN AGAINST ASHE
Nasty: Ilie Nastase vs Tennis by Richard Evans

———•·•·•———

I get angry, and the anger gives me energy. It makes things more exciting.

MARC ROSSET, ATP PLAYER, ON HIS COURT TANTRUM
www.marcrosset.com

Sometimes I get carried away and I end up making a fool of myself. In the future, I'm going to try to watch it. I'm not apologizing, I'm just saying I've made some mistakes.

JIMMY CONNORS
The Tennis Bubble by Rich Koster

———

I tried to do too many things. I just started making errors that I should not have. I started going for too much and not concentrating on keeping the ball in play.

JELENA DOKIC, WTA PLAYER, ON A MATCH SLIPPING AWAY AT WIMBLEDON (2001)

When you go on the court, look around and soak it all in, then blank it out. Once the match begins, you don't want to find yourself looking around or wondering about the place.

DOUG SPREEN, ATP TRAINER, TO ANDY RODDICK, ON HIS FIRST TIME
AT WIMBLEDON CENTRE COURT
Tennis (December 2001)

Tennis is a lot like life, working hard in a rally, exploring for openings, taking risks, making the points, missing.

CHRIS EVERT
Sports Illustrated (August 28, 1989)

After being up two sets and having a big lead in the third set and then losing that set, I lost the fourth set because he said he couldn't stop thinking about the blown set.

MAGNUS LARSON, ATP PLAYER, AT ROLAND GARROS (1997)

You never know what to expect when you're going to walk off the court with a rain delay, have to come back, basically start a new match from the beginning.

YEVGENY KAFELNIKOV, ATP PLAYER (2001)

People who think I am nice would be surprised by what goes on in my head during a match. I am a total bitch out there. If you look at my face I am the meanest person out there.

LINDSAY DAVENPORT
Venus Envy by L. Jon Wertheim

I can almost feel it coming. I am able to transport myself beyond the turmoil of the court to some place of total peace and calm. I know where the ball is on every shot and it looks as big as a basketball.

BILLIE JEAN KING, ON CONCENTRATION
The Right Set edited by Caryl Phillips

It doesn't matter what draw anybody has. You just have to focus on yourself and worry about playing good tennis.

MEGAN SHAUGHNESSY, WTA PLAYER
Palm Springs Desert Sun (March 10, 2002)

I wasn't playing for somebody, but I was always thinking, what will people think about that? What will the coach think? Now, I don't think anything. If I win I am happy. If I lose, never mind. Whatever happens, it's for me.

ANNA SMASHNOVA, WTA PLAYER
Palm Springs Desert Sun (March 12, 2002)

The Thrill of Victory . . .

I don't even care if I ever play a match again in my life.
If I don't want to play, I don't play again. This is it. This
is the end of the world.

GORAN IVANISEVIC, AFTER WINNING WIMBLEDON (2001)

———

I wasn't that focused on the match, thinking it is the
same win or lose. But after two days I realized how bad
it was to lose.

ALEX CORRETJA, ATP PLAYER, ON LOSING FINALS AT ROLAND GARROS
(2001)

Love twice cost me Wimbledon finals. Once when Connors showed up with Susan George and once when I started to see John Lloyd. I wasn't focused. I wish I had been a little tougher.

CHRIS EVERT
Sports Illustrated (August 28, 1989)

It is one thing to be able to accept success. It is far harder to take defeat. There is always another day and your good days will far outnumber the bad.

FRED PERRY
Court on Court by Margaret Court

Dreams do come true. I no longer am going to doubt myself in anything. If I can win a grand slam then I know anything is possible.

JENNIFER CAPRIATI (2001)

At times it's tough finding that motivation. The years of being number one took a lot out of me. Winning slams, being on top of the game you get to a certain point. You have to be very selective of your goals.

PETE SAMPRAS (2001)

I couldn't take the point. At the end of the day when I leave the courts and go home, I want to feel good about myself.

MAGNUS NORMAN, ON LOSING TO SEBASTIEN GROSJEAN AFTER REVERSING THE CALL ON A MATCH POINT
Tennis (February 2002)

The only language that counts on the court and in the locker room is winning. There is no one who is number one who doesn't deserve it. You don't buy your points in a supermarket.

THOMAS MUSTER
Agassi & Ecstacy by Paul Bauman

I am Wimbledon champion. I can die and nothing can change that.

GORAN IVANISEVIC (2001)

———•••••———

There are bad days, bad months. Just because you have this great win at the 2000 U.S. Open doesn't mean you are going to play great the rest of your life. You play bad and come back, just like the stock market.

MARAT SAFIN, ATP PLAYER (2001)

It's quite tough when you win Wimbledon at age seventeen. There is so much pressure and so many expectations. People thought I could overtake everyone. That was not possible.

BORIS BECKER
Fort Lauderdale Sun-Sentinel (September 11, 1989)

In 1987 I knew what I was working toward. I knew I had the ability to be number one. Maybe it came too early. But it did not come easily. Can you get beyond number one? No one has.

MATS WILANDER
Fort Lauderdale Sun-Sentinel (August 29, 1989)

I was stopped at the height of my career and I had to restart literally instead of continuing. I am here to win the tournament. That's why you play tournaments: to win.

MONICA SELES
The New York Times (September 2, 1996)

It was not a pretty sight, but somehow deep in his stricken system, Sampras found the strength to stagger back. Pale and wan, propping himself up by his racquet between the points, he literally staggered to victory.

GEORGE VECSEY, ON SAMPRAS BEATING ALEX CORRETJA
The New York Times (September 6, 1996)

That was like a dream and it was one of those matches where everything went my way. That doesn't happen very often. It's a great feeling when you can't do anything wrong.

STEFAN EDBERG, ON HIS 1991 U.S. OPEN TITLE MATCH AGAINST JIM COURIER
Fort Lauderdale Sun-Sentinel (January 25, 1992)

My attitude coming in was not of defending. I went out there and played to win instead of not to lose.

JIM COURIER, ON HIS WINNING BACK-TO-BACK FRENCH OPENS
Fort Lauderdale Sun-Sentinel (June 8, 1992)

Winning is everything to tennis players, although more than 99 percent of them are certain losers.

"CENTRE COURT" BY JOHN MCPHEE
Playboy (June 1971)

From the 1910 win at Wimbledon Tilden did not lose another match of any significance anywhere in the world for the next six years. Playing for himself, for his country, for posterity, he was invincible. No player ever before strode his sport as Tilden did in those years.

FRANK DEFORD
Big Bill Tilden

I had losses so devastating on the court I would go back to my hotel and cry . . . but you learn to cope and come back strong.

PAM SHRIVER
Venus Envy by L. Jon Wertheim

I was robbed by a man without a mask, the baselinesman was older than God—guess he was sleeping. Louise's shot was a foot long.

NANCYE WYNN BOLTON, ON LOSING SEMIS TO 1947 CHAMP LOUISE BROUGH

You think that was good?—all the eight linespeople are wrong and you are right?

> TIM HENMAN, WHEN A FAN TOLD HIM HE WAS ROBBED ON A LINE CALL (2001)

Why would I hit hard against Connors and let him eat me up with pace? He loves pace. He hates when you hit short and slow to his forehand. Does he think I am stupid because he doesn't like it or what?

> IVAN LENDL
> *Fort Lauderdale Sun Sentinel* (September 7, 1992)

Looking at Juan Carlos Ferraro you can't tell if he is winning or losing, he maintains that stoic look throughout the match.

TONY TRABERT, CBS SPORTS COMMENTATOR, 2001 U.S. OPEN

Wisdom and Advice
from the Pros

You have to save something for late in the match. You can't show your opponent everything in the beginning or he will adjust to it. If you know you have a weapon for later in the match you will have a psychological edge.

JOHN NEWCOMB
Carnival at Forest Hills by Marty Bell

There's always more to learn in this game, no matter how long you've been playing.

ROY EMERSON
The Tennis Lover's Book of Wisdom edited by Criswell Freeman

Foot speed is the most important element in men's tennis today. With the players bigger and stronger and the equipment more powerful, speed is essential.

PAT MCENROE (2001)

Tennis is not an exact science but a great emotional drama—ultimately it is a game of reduction. One player makes the other surrender.

DAVID GREY
Ken Rosewall: Twenty Years at the Top by Peter Rowley

Your feet are the point from which the footwork is done. You must be easy upon them. Do not allow them to hold the ground flatly, for then movement in any direction will not be instant—never run too fast, run with short steps.

SUZANNE LENGLEN
The Right Set edited by Caryl Phillips

How to play on clay? You go over to Europe and play for six weeks until you have clay up to your knees. You play and learn to fight for every point in every match. You learn to develop alternative game plans.

TONY TRABERT
Tennis Week (June 26, 2001)

On clay the game is based on rhythm—you have to work with the ball—footwork is the key to rhythm—having heart and physical strength also help.

TARIK BENHABILES
Tennis Week (June 26, 2001)

Players who grow up on clay know the first rule is not to miss. If you play the wrong shot on a fast surface the court forgives you. On clay you play for position—if you pull the trigger too soon you are in trouble.

JOSE HIGUERAS
Tennis Week (June 26, 2001)

Jim Courier was the first person who told me you can learn from your wins, you can learn from what you did right.

JAMES BLAKE
North Carolina Tennis Today (October 2001)

———

Your game is only as good as your second serve.

JOHN NEWCOMB
Ken Rosewall: Twenty Years at the Top by Peter Rowley

It doesn't matter what style you use, as long as you do it all the time and master it.

DAVID LUTHER
Winning Tennis by Scott Perlstein

———

When you hit big second-serve returns you place a seed of worry in the opponent's head—that often leads to double fault.

PAT MCENROE (2001)

You don't need quite so much speed if you have anticipation knowing where the ball is going to go from the memory of previous times in the same situation. Some players have this from the beginning; others improve with experience.

TORBEN ULRICH
Remembrance of Games Past by John Sharnik

A tennis match is a thousand little sprints.

BJORN BORG

One of the biggest strategy concepts I learned from Jose Higueras was to not carry the burden of the point on every shot.

Jim Courier

When you are playing a better player, you just can't throw it out there waiting for the opportunities. You must create your own opportunities.

Mal Washington (2001)

Timing, not body size, is the key to power.

MARY CARILLO

The most important skill in tennis is timing.

PANCHO SEGURA
Pancho Segura's Championship Strategy

When you are hitting the ball don't look at the court, it never moves. Don't look at the opponent, they will not be in the wrong place.

MARY CARILLO

Think in terms of four- to six-ball rallies. Make the opponent run corner to corner. Do it for three points in a row and the opponent will be baked for good.

BRAD GILBERT
Tennis (October 2001)

Sometimes you must make errors in order to make progress.

JUSTINE HENIN

When you lose your rhythm serving, it's because of a lack of concentration.

ROGER TAYLOR
"Centre Court" by John McPhee
Playboy (June 1971)

Stay with a coach until you feel he has given you all the information he has, then move on.

MARTY DAVIS
Winning Tennis by Scott Perlstein

When scouting, I look to create a picture in my mind of a player's strengths, weaknesses, and tendencies under pressure. Where does he serve on big points? Where does he hit his passing shots?

BRAD STINE, PRO COACH
USPTA magazine (December 2001)

I love scouting. It brings you into the match. There were plenty of times when I've seen a player do something under pressure that Andre Agassi could use.

BRAD GILBERT
Fort Lauderdale Sun-Sentinel (March 24, 2002)

It is the most consistent player who usually wins.

NICOLAS ESCUDE

I will have to go with a more aggressive game plan. I don't want to give up just like that. I have to find the motivation and the hunger for winning.

MARTINA HINGIS (2001)

You must come on the court with five game plans and be prepared to use all of them.

JOHN MCENROE
Winning Tennis by Scott Perlstein

To me the great volleyers are those who are in the right position—those who move better.

PAT CASH

The most important thing [smaller players] have to be able to do is neutralize power, then learn to manipulate the point so that the power isn't going to beat them.

Scott McCain, USTA coach
Fort Lauderdale Sun-Sentinel (March 20, 2002)

———

Talent is more than hitting the ball and moving well. It's being able to travel all the time, accept poor conditions and losing while you learn. It's fighting and sticking with it even when you are playing bad.

Nikki Pilic
Sampras: A Legend in the Works by H. A. Branham

There is no substitution for match play and you must take the positives from every match.

WAYNE ARTHURS

If you don't go for it, chances pass you by. I tried to go for it at important times.

GUSTAVO KUERTEN

Figure out what your opponent's weaker side is and hit every ball to that side. If you have a wide open shot to the strength side then you can go there, otherwise break down the weaker side.

TIM WILKERSON
North Carolina Tennis Today (2001)

You must take advantage of your opportunities because if you let your opponent hang around he is bound to play some good points.

JOSE HIGUERAS

In a match, visualize the times you were on the practice court in the same situation. Remove all the other elements. Then hit the ball the way you did in practice when there wasn't any pressure.

CHRIS EVERT
Tennis (October 2001)

———

You must identify your strengths and use them.

JOSE HIGUERAS

No matter how talented you are it is only possible to play good tennis through commitment to improving the technical parts of your game and your fitness.

TIM WILKERSON
North Carolina Tennis Today (2001)

It's playing on the right side of your brain. It is creative, mystical, letting your body do what it knows how to do. Logic, rationality and reasoning don't interfere.

ARTHUR ASHE, ON PLAYING IN THE ZONE
World Tennis Magazine (December 1989)

It boils down to watching the ball and executing.

ANDRE AGASSI (2001)

—•—

Hopefully you don't stop learning ever. There are always new players, always new things to think about, new elements. You've got to constantly adjust, especially as you get older.

ANDRE AGASSI
Cross Court Tennis Internet newsletter (March 24, 2002)

The problem is that when I win the first set too easily, I sometimes lose my concentration and then the other player starts to play better.

ARANTXA SANCHEZ VICARIO
Fort Lauderdale Sun-Sentinel (September 3, 1989)

A good player never misses easy ones. Remember that if you do miss a simple shot you should have made, you are giving your opponent two points. The difference between plus one and minus one.

BILL TILDEN
Big Bill Tilden by Frank Deford

I became a devotee of road work when I was young. I became convinced that the most useful form of running is a series of fifteen yards jogging and thirty yards sprinting.

HARRY HOPMAN, FORMER AUSTRALIAN DAVIS CUP COACH
Game, Set, and Match by Herbert Warren Wind

Most young players want to be too flashy. They don't realize nine good shots will beat one sensational shot. They don't think about setting up the winning shot with two or three shots that pull the opponent out of position.

HAZEL HOTCHKISS WRIGHTMAN
Game, Set, and Match by Herbert Warren Wind

My father's coaching philosophy when working with me was to be patient, be steady, let your opponent make the mistake. The player with the least errors will win the match.

CHRIS EVERT
Chrissie by Chris Evert and Neil Amdur.

Playing good defense means not only using good retrieving skills but having the patience to work a point until your opponent gives you a chance to win it.

BRAD GILBERT
Tennis (May 2002)

A service break is not a service break until you hold serve in the next game.

TIM HENMAN
Palm Springs Desert Sun (March 12, 2002)

———

You're a tennis artist and artists always know better than anybody else when they are right. If you believe in a certain way to play, you play that way no matter what anyone tells you. Be true to your art.

MARY GARDEN, FAMOUS OPERA SINGER, WHO PROVIDED BILL TILDEN
WITH THE CONCEPT OF ATHLETE-AS-ARTIST
Big Bill Tilden by Frank Deford

Confidence is like love. When you look too hard, you don't find it. When you let it come naturally, it happens.

MARAT SAFIN
*Inside Tennis (*March 2002)

———•·•·•———

In this life you are as you play.

MELANIE MOLITOR, COACH AND MOTHER OF MARTINA HINGIS
(2001)

I use tennis as a tool. I use it for teaching responsibility . . . that's all this is about. It's not about saving the nation—it's about helping kids one at a time. Tennis is the way I do that.

BARBARA LEWIS, HEAD OF THE RICHMOND YOUTH TENNIS CENTER
Northern California Tennis Newsletter (November 2001)

Talent is great, but hard work is even better.

RICHARD KRAJICEK
www.richardkrajicek.com

Champions are not born, they are made. They emerge from a long, hard school of defeat, discouragement and mediocrity not because they were born tennis players but they are endowed with a force that transcends discouragement and cries, "I will succeed."

BILL TILDEN
Tennis: Nostalgia by Christopher Dunkley

———

The fifth set has nothing to do with tennis. It is all about heart and fighting.

BORIS BECKER

Ranking points don't lie. You have to earn every single one of them.

TIM HENMAN (1998)

Tennis is one of the few things in life you can't fake how good you are.

PANCHO SEGURA
Tennis Week (February 13, 2001)

What makes a champion? Giving up the enjoyment of
life for the sake of practice.

PANCHO GONZALEZ
Tough Draw by Eliot Berry

There is a point in every match when the match can be
had. Even when a player is down, there is usually one
chance, one moment to get back into it or fade away.

STEFAN EDBERG
Tough Draw by Eliot Berry

There are no good or bad draws. You have to make it good.

BORIS BECKER

There are five days a year you will beat everyone, five days a year you will beat no one. All the rest are what makes a great tennis player.

BRAD GILBERT
Agassi & Ecstasy by Paul Bauman

In tennis less is more, more is much less.

FRANK FANNING, COACH

———•••———

Being a good server is more than aces. It's placement, spin patterns and first-serve percentile.

MAL WASHINGTON
ESPN (April 5, 2002)

No player has A+ strengths on all of the skills. Not even the very top pros. The game is about how you use your strengths and defend your weaknesses.

PAT MCENROE
ESPN (February 24, 2002)

You can't win a grand slam in the first week, but you can lose it.

BRAD GILBERT

THE QUOTABLE TENNIS PLAYER

Unforgettable Moments

Nothing to apologize for. Nothing to question. Two sisters beat incredible odds, played the 2001 Open finals in prime time and just for that they deserve universal praise and respect.

HARVEY ARATON, ON THE WILLIAMS SISTERS' FINALS
The New York Times (September 9, 2001)

I never planned on breaking Roy Emerson's twelve grand slam victories. It kind of transcended into something that I put myself in a position to do. It's amazing.

PETE SAMPRAS
The New York Times (July 10, 2000)

To appreciate and understand what Sampras has accomplished, you have to love tennis, understand tennis. He is Hank Aaron not Babe Ruth, Joe Louis, Muhammad Ali, Jack Nicklaus, not Tiger Woods. To break the record, Sampras played a grinding, grueling game. No flash. Terribly efficient.

WILLIAM RHODEN, ON PETE SAMPRAS'S RECORD GRAND SLAM
The New York Times (July 10, 2001)

I knew it was something that really touched the people when I did it the first time. The second time I was so full of good things and happiness that I wanted to share it with the people around me.

GUSTAVO KUERTEN, ON TWICE DRAWING A HEART ON THE COURT AFTER HIS VICTORY, ROLAND GARROS (2001)

The man that stabbed me took a lot away from me . . . some great years, some grand slam wins. It was a nightmare. I'm never going to be the same, but I think I am still lucky to be playing tennis. If the knife had plunged a half millimeter to the left, I would be paralyzed and in a wheelchair.

MONICA SELES
The New York Times (September 7, 1998)

I don't know how long I can play. Because of the injury I've had pulled muscles, shin splints, and every day I spend two hours in the training room—it's no fun.

THOMAS MUSTER, FRENCH OPEN CHAMPION, ON HIS COMEBACK
AFTER AN ACCIDENT INVOLVING A CAR ROLLING ONTO HIS LEGS
Fort Lauderdale Sun-Sentinel (September 9, 1991)

How long does it take to stop worrying about an injury? It took me six months before I could completely forget.

CEDRIC PIOLINE, ATP PLAYER AT ROLAND GARROS (2001), AFTER
RECOVERY FROM A HAND INJURY

Bruno Rebeuh showed favoritism in matches. I never had a chair umpire behave so badly.

> JEFF TARANGO, ATP PLAYER, AFTER WALKING OFF THE COURT DURING
> HIS WIMBLEDON MATCH, FOLLOWED BY HIS WIFE, WHO SLAPPED THE
> CHAIR UMPIRE
> *The New York Times* (June 25, 1997)

I had hit the shot of my life to beat the Wimbledon champ in my home country—may never happen again. I see the ball hitting the net cord in my dreams every day.

> DERRICK ROSTAGNO, FORMER ATP PLAYER, ON HIS MATCH POINT
> AGAINST BORIS BECKER, WHEN BECKER HIT A VOLLEY WINNER OFF A
> NET CORD SHOT HIT AND WENT ON TO WIN THE MATCH AND THE
> TOURNAMENT
> *Hard Courts* by John Feinstein

Without provocation some 20,000 people rose to their feet in the Arthur Ashe Stadium standing to honor greatness during the 2001 Sampras–Agassi match.

BRUCE JENKINS, U.S. OPEN 2001
San Francisco Chronicle

I learned to compete from Serena. There was a match in which she was way down against a higher ranked player and came back. From that day on I grew a bigger heart.

VENUS WILLIAMS (2001)

I will always respect you as a player but never again as a man.

> STAN SMITH, TO ION TIRIAC, AFTER SMITH BEAT TIRIAC AT THE 1972
> DAVIS CUP MATCH WITH ROMANIA, WHERE CHEATING BY LOCAL OFFI-
> CIALS WAS BLATANT
> *Days of Grace: A Memoir* by Arthur Ashe

The two-plus years of being out robbed her worse than the World War II years robbed Budge, Kramer and von Cramm. What made matters worse—Guenter Parche, the person who stabbed her—was that the German court determined he was not a danger to anyone else and let him go free.

> PETER SEDDON, ON MONICA SELES BEING STABBED
> *Tennis Week* (March 7, 2002)

The underhand serve can be a tactic but in Hingis's case it seemed like it was the parting shot of her breakdown. It's like she used the serve out of spite because she didn't want Steffi to win in a normal way. She acted like a defiant teenager.

PAM SHRIVER, FORMER PLAYER AND NOW ESPN COMMENTATOR, ON HINGIS SERVING UNDERHAND TWICE IN THE LAST GAME OF THE FINALS AT THE 1999 FRENCH OPEN
Robin Finn, *The New York Times* (June 20, 1999)

I saw Vines swing his racquet and I heard the ball hit the back canvas. The umpire called game, set and match so I knew it was over but I never saw the ball.

BUNNY AUSTIN, ON ELLSWORTH VINES'S MATCH POINT WIN AT
WIMBLEDON IN 1932
Bud Collins' Modern Encyclopedia of Tennis by Bud Collins

Shots that would have stood out vividly in the average match were commonplace in the cascade of electrifying strokes that stemmed from the racquets of two superb fighters until the onlookers were fairly surfeited with brilliance.

ALLISON DANZIG, ON THE DON BUDGE–VON CRAMM DAVIS CUP MATCH IN 1938
The History of the Davis Cup by Alan Trengove

The match was a bullfight without a matador; a prize fight without a punch being thrown between Thomas Muster, the surly man who insists he never called Agassi a poor man's Pete Sampras, and Andre Agassi, the glib man, who insists he never called Muster a second-rate number one.

ROBIN FINN
The New York Times (September 5, 1996)

I spent my whole career trying to get crowds to sound like basketball or football crowds. For those eleven days it happened. I was in the eye of the hurricane and everyone was getting caught in the wind around me.

JIMMY CONNORS, ON HIS 1991 RUN TO THE SEMIS
The New York Times (July 12, 1998)

I decided to come to the net until the cows come home.

PETE SAMPRAS, ON HIS MATCH WITH MIKHAIL YOUZHNY, U.S. OPEN 2001

Bibliography

Artnon, Elaine, ed. *The Quotable Woman.* New York: Facts on File, 2001.

Ashe, Arthur. *Days of Grace: A Memoir.* New York: Ballantine Books, 1994.

Bauman, Paul. *Agassi & Ecstasy: The Turbulent Life of Andre Agassi.* Chicago: Bonus Books, 1997.

Bell, Catherine, and Roy Peters. *Passing Shots: The Path to Tennis Glory.* Glencaple, Scotland: Beaufort Books, 1983.

Bell, Marty. *Carnival at Forest Hills.* New York: Random House, 1975.

Berry, Eliot. *Tough Draw.* New York: Henry Holt & Co., 1992.

Branham, H. A. *Sampras: A Legend in the Works.* Chicago: Bonus Books, 1996.

Collins, Bud, ed. *The Best American Sports Writing 2000.* New York: Houghton-Mifflin, 2000.

Collins, Bud, ed. *The Best American Sports Writing 2001.* New York: Houghton-Mifflin, 2001.

Collins, Bud. *Bud Collins' Modern Encyclopedia of Tennis.* Canton, Mich.: Visible Ink Press, 1997.

Collins, Bud. *My Life with the Pros.* New York: Dutton, 1989.

Cummings, Parke. *American Tennis.* Boston: Little, Brown & Co., 1957.

Deford, Frank. *The Best of Frank Deford.* Chicago: Triumph Books, 2000.

Doren, Kim and Charlie Jones. *You Go Girl!* Kansas City: Andrews McMeel Publishers, 2000.

Dunkley, Christopher. *Tennis: Nostalgia, Playing the Game.* New York: Rizzoli International, 1988.

Engelmann, Larry. *The Goddess and the American Girl.* London: Oxford University Press, 1988.

Evans, Richard. *Nasty: Ilie Nastase vs Tennis.* New York: Stein Day Publishers, 1979.

Evans, Richard. *Tales on the Court.* London: Sidgwick & Jackson, 1983.

Evert, Chris, with Neil Amdur. *Chrissie: My Own Story.* New York: Simon & Schuster, 1982.

Feinstein, John. *Hard Courts.* New York: Villard Books, 1991.

Fraser, Antonia. *Marie Antoinette: The Journey.* New York: Doubleday, 2001.

Freeman, Criswell, ed. *The Tennis Lover's Book of Wisdom.* Nashville: Grove Press, 1997.

Garner, Joe. *And the Crowd Goes Wild.* 1999. Naperville, Ill. Sourcebooks, Inc., 1999.

Groppel, Jack L. *The Corporate Athlete: How to Achieve Maximal Performance in Business and Life.* New York: John Wiley & Sons, 2000.

Halberstam, David, ed. *The Best American Sports Writing of the Century.* New York: Houghton-Mifflin, 1999.

Haylett, John and Richard Evans. *Illustrated Encyclopedi of Tennis.* New York: Exeter Books, 1989.

King, Billie Jean, Fred Stolle, with Greg Huffman. *How to Play Mixed Doubles.* New York: Simon & Schuster, 1980.

Koster, Rich. *The Tennis Bubble: Big-Money Tennis, How It Grew, and Where It's Going.* New York: Times Books, 1976.

Kriplen, Nancy. *Dwight Davis: The Man and the Cup.* London: Ebury Press, 1993.

Laver, Rod, and Roy Emerson, with Barry Tardhis. *Tennis for the Bloody Fun of It.* New York: Times Books, 1976.

Lichtenstein, Grace. *A Long Way, Baby: Behind the Scenes of Women's Pro Tennis.* New York: Vintage, 1973.

Mawrence, Amanda. *Anna Kournikova.* London: Carlton Books, 2001.

Mewshaw, Michael. *Ladies of the Court.* New York: Crown, 1993.

Mewshaw, Michael. *Short Circuit.* New York: Atheneum, 1983.

Miller, Calvin Craig. *Pete Sampras.* Greensboro, N.C.: Morgan Reynolds, 1998.

Minton, Robert. *Forest Hills: An Illustrated History.* New York: J. B. Lippincott Publishers, 1975.

Oxford Dictionary of Humorous Quotations. New York: Oxford University Press, 1995.

Perlstein, Scott. *Winning Tennis.* New York: The Lyons Press, 1999.

Phillips, Caryl, ed. *The Right Set: A Tennis Anthology.* New York: Vintage Books, 1997.

Rowley, Peter, with Ken Rosewall. *Ken Rosewall: Twenty Years at the Top.* New York: G.P. Putnam's Sons, 1976.

Segura, Pancho, with Gladys Heldman. *Pancho Segura's Championship Strategy.* New York: McGraw-Hill, 1976.

Sharnik, John. *Remembrnace of Games Past: On Tour with the Tennis Grand Masters.* New York: MacMillan, 1986.

Simmons, Cindy Brinker. *Little Mo's Legacy: A Mother's Lessons, A Daughter's Story.* Irving, Texas: Tapestry Press, 2001.

Slater, Robert. *Great Jews In Sports.* Middle Village, N.Y.: Jonathan David Publishers, 1993.

Smith, Margaret Court, with George McGann. *Court on Court, a Life in Tennis.* New York: Cornwall Press, 1975.

Tauziat, Natalie. *Les Dessous du Tennis Feminin.* Paris: Plum Publishers, 2001.

Treasury of Modern Quotations from Reader's Digest. New York: Thomas Crowell Co., 1975.

Trengove, Alan. *The Story of the Davis Cup.* London: Stanley Paul, 1985.

United States Lawn Tennis Association Official Encyclopedia of Tennis. New York: Harper and Row, 1972.

Wertheim, L. Jon. *Venus Envy: A Sensational Season Inside the Women's Tennis Tour.* New York: HarperCollins, 2001.

Wind, Herbert Warren. *Game, Set and Match.* New York: Dutton, 1979.

Wolf, Warner. *Let's Go to the Videotape!* New York: Penguin Putnam, 2000.

Index

Abe, Julia, 52
Adams, Katherine, 219
Adams, Susan B., 14
Agassi, Andre, 14, 150, 164, 203, 205, 286
Agden, Kristin, 164
Alsonso, Manuel, 94
Amdur, Neil, 33, 82, 145, 154, 167, 174, 184
Anchevski, Jennifer, 23
Annacone, Paul, 138, 201
Anonymous (Wimbledon official), 15
Anonymous (young European player), 107
Anthony, Julie, 232
Araton, Harvey, 90, 190, 301
Arias, Jimmy, 193
Arthurs, Wayne, 95, 282
Ashe, Arthur, 127, 143, 285
Austin, Bunny, 11, 309
Austin, Tracy, 157

Barker, Sue, 108
Beainy, Stan, 111
Becker, Boris, 14, 258, 293, 296
Beers, Ken, 101
Bell, Catherine, 72, 75, 162, 168, 174

Bell, Marty, 62, 220
Benhabiles, Tarik, 270
Berger, Jay, 170
Berra, Yogi, 102
Berry, Eliot, 62
Bigliardi, Naomi, 107
Bitti, Francisco Ricci, 10
Black, Justice Hugo, 99
Blake, James, 271
Bodo, Peter, 95, 159
Bolton, Nancy Wynn, 262
Borg, Bjorn, 178, 189, 273
Borotra, Jean, 53
Bouin, Philippe, 154
Bradley, Ed, 22
Branham, H. A., 134, 163
Brinker, Charles, 37, 176, 182
Brinker-Simmons, Cindy, 171, 218
Brock, Tony, 91
Brough, Louise, 180
Brusteaghi, Gabriella, 69
Buckholtz, Cliff, 188
Burton, Angela, 200

Cannon, Jimmy, 103
Capriati, Jennifer, 55, 146, 147, 156, 198, 255

Carillo, Mary, 105, 191, 196, 275
Carson, Johnny, 115
Carter, President Jimmy, 44
Casals, Rosie, 198
Cash, Pat, 280
Chatrier, Philippe, 81
Cheney, Dodo, 45, 114
Chesnokov, Andre, 119
Clarey, Christopher, 180
Clemenceau, Georges, 233
Clement, Arnaud, 240
Clinton, President Bill, 78
Collins, Bud, 16, 80, 117, 153, 192, 199
Connors, Gloria Thompson, 143
Connors, Jimmy, 63, 224, 246, 311
Cooke, Alistair, 21
Corretja, Alex, 31, 113, 147, 253
Cosell, Howard, 23, 26
Courier, Jim, 222, 260, 274
Court, Margaret Smith, 17, 168
Cummings, Parke, 7, 8
Curren, Kevin, 134

Danzig, Allison, 172, 310
Davenport, Lindsay, 38, 87, 126, 156,
    207, 249
Davis, Marty, 57, 80, 122, 128, 277
De Picciotto, Phil, 85
Deford, Frank, 70, 71, 72, 261

Dent, Taylor, 179, 219
Dodge, Larry, 76
Dokic, Jelena, 109, 246
Drysdale, Cliff, 40, 163, 167, 179, 186
Dunkley, Christopher, 5
Dupuis, Anthony, 240

Edberg, Stefan, 12, 260, 295
Emerson, Roy, 71, 267
Enberg, Dick, 155, 159
Escude, Nicolas, 279
Evans, Richard, 9, 18, 79, 110, 184, 210
Evert, Chris, 16, 29, 39, 169, 190, 197,
    208, 211, 221, 241, 247, 254,
    284, 289
Fanning, Frank, 297
Federer, Roger, 204, 236
Feinstein, John, 201
Fernandez, Mary Jo, 40
Fink, Steve, 153, 175
Finn, John, 239
Finn, Robin, 138, 311
Firlus, Robert, 173
Fitzgerald, John, 123
Forget, Guy, 56
Fox, Allen, 244
Fraser, Antonia, 6
Frawley, Rod, 158
Frost, Robert, 100

Galbraith, Pat, 67
Gambill, Jan Michael, 79
Garden, Mary, 290
Garner, Joe, 22
Gaudio, Gaston, 228
Gilmour, William, 52
Gilbert, Brad, 204, 205, 276, 278, 289, 296, 298
Godfree, Kitty, 51
Goldblatt, Art, 48
Gonzalez, Pancho, 70, 137, 295
Goolagong, Evonne, 43
Graf, Steffi, 74
Graham, Sen. Bob, 231
Graham, Debra, 58
Graham, Virginia, 99
Greenwald, Jeff, 232
Grey, David, 268
Groppel, Jack, 45, 46, 238
Gullikson, Tim, 127, 195, 214, 218
Gumble, Bryant, 144

Habsudova, Karina, 50
Harper's Weekly, 8
Harris, Hank, 188
Hart, Doris, 17, 189
Henin, Justine, 59, 220, 276
Henman, Tim, 35, 106, 131, 213, 229, 263, 290, 294

Hewitt, Lleyton, 208
Higueras, Jose, 91, 270, 283, 284
Hingis, Martina, 36, 139, 279
Hoffman, Darrell, 176
Holak, Betsy, 237
Hopman, Harry, 288
Humperdinck, Engelbert, 105
Hunt, Lamar, 20

Ivanisevic, Goran, 109, 148, 223, 225, 253, 257

Jenkins, Bruce, 73, 160, 306
Jenkins, Sally, 161
Jensen, Luke, 110
Johansson, Thomas, 195

Kafelnikov, Yevgeny, 123, 200, 248
Kilborn, Craig, 114
King, Billie Jean, 18, 73, 102, 136, 249
Kipling, Rudyard, 135
Kournikova, Anna, 60, 75
Krajicek, Richard, 292
Kramer, Jack, 24, 88
Krasnoroutskaya, Lina, 165
Krickstein, Aaron, 36
Kriese, Chuck, 217
Krishnan, Ramanathan, 83
Kuerten, Gustavo, 282, 303

Lacoste, Rene, 144, 187
Larson, Magnus, 248
Laver, Rod, 20, 54, 100, 132
Leand, Andrea, 9
Lee, Martin, 226, 235
Lendl, Ivan, 31, 89, 242, 243, 263
Lenglen, Suzanne, 269
Letterman, David, 125
Levering, Judy, 25
Lewis, Barbara, 292
Lichtenstein, Grace, 172, 173
Lieberman, Nancy, 39
Lipsyte, Robert, 24, 68, 185
Loehr, Jim, 33, 63, 227
Luther, David, 272

MacKay, Barry, 21
McCain, Scott, 281
McEnroe, John, 85, 86, 116, 121, 124, 202, 224, 280
McEnroe, Pat, 152, 268, 272, 298
McManus, Sean, 19
McMillan, Frew, 165
McPhee, John, 131, 169, 261
Mandlikova, Hana, 38
Marble, Alice, 199
Marmion, Harry, 12
Martin, Todd, 207
Martinez, Cece, 231

Martinez, Conchita, 126
Marx, Harpo, 104
Maunupau, Lou, 77
Medvedev, Andrei, 32, 225, 241
Merlo, Henry, 13
Mewshaw, Michael, 120, 145
Miller, Calvin Craig, 202
Minton, Robert, 13, 67, 192
Molitor, Melanie, 291
Molly, John F., 238
Moody, Helen Wills, 49
Murray, Jim, 183
Muscutel, Cyndy, 5
Muster, Thomas, 256, 304
Myers, A. Wallis, 133

Nastase, Ilie, 237, 245
Navratilova, Martina, 146, 243
Newcomb, John, 125, 267, 271
Noah, Yannick, 47
Norman, Magnus, 256

O'Neill, Paul, 60
Ostler, Scott, 166

Paes, Leander, 30, 48, 61
Paolantonio, Sal, 150
Papp, Frank, 50
Parsons, John, 152

Pasarell, Charlie, 76
Paz, Antony, 230
Pelic, Nikki, 281
Perry, Fred, 11, 254
Peters, Roy, 72, 75, 162, 168, 174
Philippoussis, Mark, 35, 56
Pioline, Cedric, 226, 230, 304
Potter, Barbara, 140
Pucin, Diane, 93, 155
Purcell, Mel, 96

Rafter, Patrick, 106, 112
Razzano, Virginia, 217
Rhoden, William, 302
Right Set: A Tennis Anthology, The
   (Phillips, ed.), 74
Ritzenberg, Allie, 104
Roberts, Selena, 149, 166
Robinson, Ted, 178
Roche, Tony, 206
Rochus, Oliver, 242
Roddick, Andy, 78, 194, 196, 203
Rogers, Keith, 157
Ross, Tom, 59, 175
Rosset, Marc, 245
Rostagno, Derrick, 305
Rowley, Peter, 115, 177

Safin, Marat, 112, 148, 257, 291

Sampras, Pete, 53, 55, 133, 135, 197,
   206, 212, 255, 301, 312
Santana, Carlos, 57
Santoro, Fabrice, 244
Sarni, Jim, 137, 181, 191, 209
Schnyder, Patty, 228
Scott, Eugene L., 10, 130
Seddon, Peter, 307
Segura, Pancho, 275, 294
Seles, Monica, 34, 259, 303
Shakespeare, William, 7
Sharnik, John, 128
Shaughnessy, Megan, 250
Shiras, Leif, 223
Shriver, Pam, 118, 262, 308
Simons, William C., 61, 162
Slater, Robert, 170
Slater, Stephanie, 183
Smashnova, Anna, 250
Smith, Col. Jackie, 117
Smith, Stan, 307
Solomon, Harold, 49
Spreen, Doug, 247
Stahl, Joseph, 181
Stefanki, Steve, 29
Stevenson, Alexandra, 31, 37
Stine, Brad, 84, 278
Stolle, Fred, 30, 34, 102, 111, 177
Sugiyama, Ai, 213

Sun, The (London tabloid), 158

Talbert, Bill, 19, 68
Tarango, Jeff, 305
Tardhis, Barry, 121
Tauziat, Natalie, 69
Taylor, Roger, 277
*Tennis Lover's Book of
    Wisdom, The* (Freeman, ed.), 113
Tilden, Bill, 229, 287, 293
Tingay, Lance, 103
Tinling, Ted, 92
Trabert, Tony, 264, 269
Trengrove, Alan, 194

Ulrich, Torben, 273
Unger, Jeff, 124
*United States Lawn Tennis Association
    Official Encyclopedia of Tennis*,
    93, 193

Van Allen, Jimmy, 81
Vecsey, George, 15, 87, 88, 151, 259

Vicario, Arantxa Sanchez, 119, 287
Wade, Virginia, 64
Washington, Mali Vai, 86, 222,
    274, 297
Webster, John, 101
Wehls, Vanessa, 234
Wertheim, L. Jon, 122
Wheaton, David, 118
Whitford, Bradford, 47
Wilander, Mats, 116, 258
Wilkerson, Tim, 283, 285
Williams, Oracen, 40
Williams, Serena, 149, 221, 234
Williams, Venus, 51, 139, 306
Wimbledon official (anonymous), 15
Wind, Herbert Warren, 185
Wolfe, Warner, 161
Woodell, Karen, 82
Woodruff, Chris, 239
Wrightman, Hazel Hotchkiss, 288
Wuoff, Kevin, 83

Yannick, Noah, 89